MW00791807

Praise for *Culture Built My Brand*

Brands without a thriving internal culture are zombie brands. They may not know it, but they're dead inside. Culture Built My Brand *will teach you how to bring your organization's culture to life in ways that fuel success and performance.*

Jim Moriarty, Co Managing Director, Brand Citizens

For leaders looking to nurture, change, or turn around their culture, Ted and Mark's work in Culture Built My Brand *offers practical advice, real-life examples, and a road map to align your culture with your brand.*

Linda Rutherford, CCO, Southwest Airlines

Historic Agency has been a wonderful asset to our company. Their dedication to clients and project success is unparalleled. Culture Built My Brand *unpacks the tools and process they utilize to turn a company's culture into a magnet for new customers.*

Roger Love, Celebrity Vocal Coach & Best-Selling Author

The largest swing vote in a successful brand is the employees and culture behind it. Culture Built My Brand *is for leaders who want to shape that culture and empower their staff. Read this book!*

Kyle Buckett, Retired Navy SEAL, Executive, Author

As a student of corporate culture for nearly 40 years and a leader/ consultant for 30 of those, I've collected a lot of books and articles about this topic. Mark and Ted have managed to create some truly new perspectives and unique tools to tie your culture and brand together.

Dusty Rubeck, President & CEO, CDF Capital

Historic has the unique ability to create content marketing strategies that are custom-fit for nonprofits and also drive generosity and trust in communities. Culture Built My Brand *takes their branded content playbook and applies it to your company culture.*

Gabe Cooper, CEO, Virtuous

I have seen firsthand the incredible benefit that their firm brings to an organization. Ted and Mark's work in Culture Built My Brand *beautifully captures the critical importance of an organization's culture and how it dictates not only daily operations, both internally and externally, but how employee behavior and engagement is shaped and transformed.*

Roger Beless, COO, Streetlights

We continue to implement the cultural strategies that Historic has helped us to develop. Culture Built My Brand *will revolutionize the way you acquire customers, all thanks to your company culture.*

Todd Austin, CEO, Clark

Every company has a culture, whether or not it is defined often determines the success. Culture Built My Brand *helps business leaders create a culture that is worthy of the vision they have for their company.*

Ryan Sisson, Founder, Moniker

I have had the privilege of experiencing firsthand how Ted and Mark have transformed organizational cultures with cutting-edge branding; and now to have their insights available in print makes this a must-read for all leaders.

Dr. Mickey Stonier, National Emergency Response Chaplain

www.amplifypublishing.com

Culture Built My Brand

For more information, please contact:
Amplify Publishing, an imprint of Mascot Books
620 Herndon Parkway, Suite 320
Herndon, VA 20170
info@amplifypublishing.com

Library of Congress Control Number: 2021909460

CPSIA Code: PBANG0921A

ISBN-13: 978-1-63755-141-7

Printed in the United States

Culture Ate Built My Brand

The secret to winning more customers through company culture.

Mark Miller   **Ted Vaughn**

Contents

Foreword

Linda Rutherford

Southwest Airlines founder Herb Kelleher used to tell stories to newly hired employees to get them excited about the job they'd just accepted. He'd tell them they'd just joined "the flight of their lives." He always said we hire for attitude and train for skills. "It's not just a career, it's a cause. Our most important customers are our own employees. If you treat them right, then they will treat our external customers right," Herb would preach.

As the Dallas-based airline celebrates fifty years in 2021, Herb's "sermon" is still something all new hires are steeped in, because we know that the people of Southwest Airlines are the ones who created and who continue to nurture one of the most studied cultures in corporate America. Herb instinctively knew this when he'd tell others that "our People Department [HR] isn't just filling slots—it's building a culture."

Early on, finding just the right people—and then taking good care of them—would be a central theme in Southwest's brand. Executives focus as much on how to celebrate and reward workers as on schedule strategy and fleet planning. Over time, we realized championing guidelines over rules; maintaining flexibility and forgiveness with people; allowing people to be themselves; and using the word LOVE (or LUV, to stay true to our NYSE stock ticker symbol) in the workplace were intangibles that were even more important than the tangibles to our success.

Empowering people to live out the brand promise without too many rules, training them and trusting them to make good decisions, and emphasizing teamwork over tribalism has been part of the secret sauce that lets Southwest stand out among its airline competitors.

For leaders looking to nurture, change, or turn around their culture, Ted and Mark's work in *Culture Built My Brand* offers practical advice, real-life examples, and a road map to align your culture with your brand, ensure you have the right servant leaders steering the ship, allow your employees to live out your organization's purpose, and turn your firm's fans into fanatics.

Their client work and examples show us that strong, vibrant cultures attract talent, drive innovation, and can boost bottom-line results. But culture doesn't just happen. It takes work. You have to prioritize it. You have to invest in it.

Herb used to say that the Southwest culture was like a mosaic, made up of a thousand tiny things that come together in just the right way. In this book, Ted and Mark will introduce you to the Marquee Culture method that is equal parts art and science. They'll eloquently walk you through the science part of the effort; the art part is up to you and your leadership team, but in the pages within, they will show you what it will take to bring that effort to life. Enjoy the read, and then get to work!

Linda Rutherford
Senior Vice President and Chief Communications Officer
Southwest Airlines

Introduction

How We Got Here

[Mark]

"I think we need to change our name," said the CEO of ▇▇▇▇▇.

But that much we already knew. The organization's name, which had been chosen by the founders nearly fifty years earlier, included a word that needed to go. It had been hijacked by social forces and redefined into something negative. ▇▇▇▇▇'s senior leadership didn't want to be associated with that definition. Neither did consumers. With a name and a visual identity alienating its customer base, ▇▇▇▇▇ was struggling to convert prospects into customers and falling further behind the competition.

Our team at Historic Agency, a strategy and design firm, ran surveys and focus groups with our new client's current and potential customers. All the data came back indicating that if ▇▇▇▇▇ didn't change its name soon, it would continue to lose traction. We walked ▇▇▇▇▇'s CEO and his leadership team through our unique naming process. After testing several name options with consumers, we had a clear winner. We pulled together the data and prepared our proposal. I went out and got a new suit, put it on, and walked into the board meeting to pitch the rebrand, new name and all. It went great. The CEO loved the name and visual identity. Board members asked insightful questions, and I addressed their concerns. By the end of the meeting, everyone was smiling. The room buzzed with confidence, and the board gave us the green light to put the rebrand into action.

[Ted]

Underneath their excitement, ▇▇▇▇▇ had a big problem: the primary driver of its culture was risk mitigation. For decades, the organization had been hiring cautious leaders and training them to avoid taking chances at all costs. Now the executive team faced two competing threats: either navigate the uncertainty of renaming the organization or keep the name, slowly bleed out customers, and end up with a poorly performing brand that, while fatal, at least felt familiar. After spending $100,000 on the rebranding process, the CEO decided to scrap the new name and settle for the slow decline of the brand. The organization is still in decline today.

What happened? ████████'s CEO, executives, and board members could see their brand was disintegrating. They knew something needed to shift, and they felt excited about the new direction we offered. But their culture prevented them from knowing how to navigate uncertainty and adopt the changes that would have allowed them to reinvent their brand. At the eleventh hour, they caved to their risk-averse culture.

Mark and I have seen issues like these play out dozens of times. Executives feel the winds of change and see the need to pivot, but the weaknesses in their organizational culture undermine their ability to see the threats, much less execute the necessary changes.

No organization has failed because of its logo. But many have failed because of their internal culture. If you neglect your culture, it will turn into the ultimate internal barrier that prevents breakthrough and works against innovation. It will devour your brand.

[Mark & Ted]

WHAT'S HOLDING BACK YOUR BRAND

If you're like most leaders, you envision more for your brand. You see where it is now, and it's not where you want it to be. Something is holding it back. Performance is mediocre, and your brand is dragging behind the competition. You may notice increasing customer complaints despite rolling out new training to improve service. Perhaps your marketing efforts aren't gaining traction. Internal confusion, lack of motivation, and sideways energy are plaguing your team and draining your momentum. Employees are quitting, and you're afraid of losing even more of your best talent.

These pain points trace back to your culture. They highlight the gaps between where your brand is currently and where you want it to go. You've tried to close those gaps with fail-safe fixes touted by industry experts. But the traditional solutions haven't done enough to boost your brand.

Those standard remedies fail, not because they're bad solutions, but because they don't address the underlying problem of a misaligned internal culture blocking your brand's momentum. If you don't address that misalignment, your culture will continue threatening your success until you wake up one day and find it taking a chunk out of your backside.

THE POWER OF BRAND AND CULTURE ALIGNMENT

How your brand operates on the inside is more important than how it looks on the outside. Your internal culture—how your employees communicate and behave—defines your brand more than your logo or website. Your culture is your brand strategy.

Out of the hundreds of rebrands we've done, those that failed all followed the same pattern: their leaders ignored their internal culture until it sabotaged their brand. Meanwhile, our clients who sail through the rebranding process with success do so with a culture that lines up to support the brand and drive it forward.

We've helped organizations of every type—nonprofits and for-profits, boutique businesses and large corporations—harness their culture to build unstoppable brands. The good news is that you can do it, too.

CREATING A MARQUEE CULTURE FOR AN IRRESISTIBLE BRAND

Imagine having a culture that can:

- equip and empower your staff to consistently deliver on your brand promise through amazing products, services, and experiences;

- turn your employees into your greatest brand advocates by helping them feel more deeply invested in the brand's values and vision;

- align your organizational systems and structures to serve and empower the people they're designed to support;

- create experiences that energize and inspire your team and reinforce what's most important about your brand;

- cultivate compelling stories of brand impact that echo through the halls of your office; and

- turn your brand's differentiated ways of doing things into second nature for anyone at any level of your organization.

This type of company culture is what separates a brand from the rest. It attracts tribes of followers inside and out—not just because the brand delivers on its promise, but also because everything the organization does comes together to create an irresistible experience for both employees and customers.

That's a Marquee Culture—when your brand integrates into everything you do and, as a result, you deliver something great. Like a brightly lit sign, a Marquee Culture makes a huge promise and offers something big to draw people in. It's intentionally designed to stand out and be loud.

Your culture is the most visible, recognizable sign of your brand. And when done right, it makes a big statement about who you are and what your audience can expect from you. With a Marquee Culture guiding everything you and your people do, you create a stand-out brand that drives ahead of the competition.

A ROAD MAP FOR BRAND AND CULTURE ALIGNMENT

This book helps you build a Marquee Culture that showcases your brand. It gives you practical steps and hands-on tools to integrate each layer of your culture so your people can deliver on a promise that's true to who you are. Before you dive in, visit culturebuiltmybrand.com/tools to download materials you'll use to work through the exercises at the end of each chapter. With the right culture, you'll create lift for your brand so that it draws more customers and turns them into raving fans.

Part One provides you with a foundational understanding of brand and culture. In the first chapter, Mark shares how organizations are only as profitable as their internal culture allows them to be. He explains how leaders often ignore culture and wind up trying to solve the wrong problems. You'll learn what it takes to build a culture that awakens your external audience and turns them into your biggest brand ambassadors.

In chapter 2, Ted shares why keeping your brand promise matters. He outlines the patterns we've observed in successful brands and how they align the layers of their culture to unleash greater results. Then he lays the groundwork for building a Marquee Culture that attracts loyal fans and followers. Ted also walks you through a customizable tool to help you gain a deeper understanding of your brand.

In Part Two, we offer a practical road map for developing a Marquee Culture by integrating your brand into the six layers of your culture. We begin with Principles, the foundational values that articulate what matters most to your brand. Then we help you align the other layers of your culture, including Architecture, Rituals, Lore, and Vocabulary. We wrap it up with Artifacts, the final layer and the most visible part of your brand. These layers combine to create a culture that attracts more customers and accelerates success.

Throughout this book, you'll discover hands-on tools for dealing with drag on your culture and brand. Each chapter closes with practical tips and straightforward steps to build a culture that drives your brand's success. You'll also discover real-world examples showcasing how brands of every type and size align their culture to generate momentum. We'll show you the habits of the greatest brands of our time and combine them with everything we've learned working with hundreds of clients. After reading this book, you'll have the know-how you need to tap into your culture to lift your brand and maximize results.

We also address your leadership and organizational health, but this isn't a book on either of those topics. It's about how everything in your organization—including your leadership and organizational health—fits into the context of your culture to impact your brand. Good leadership and health are minimum standards for your organization. Our goal is to help you optimize these baselines so they align with your brand to elevate your performance and produce better outcomes.

HOW WE GOT HERE

[Ted]

I've been an entrepreneur since I was old enough to walk. When I was growing up in Orange County, California, my family had a freakishly healthy cherry tomato plant. It would not stop producing amazing cherry tomatoes. At the age of ten, I put them into plastic baggies and went door to door selling them to my neighbors for fifty cents a bag. I made a good chunk of change selling those cherry tomatoes. That entrepreneurial mindset has driven me forward in every role and job I've had since.

Recommended Healthy Culture Books

The Five
Dysfunctions
of a Team
by Patrick Lencioni

Organizational
Culture and
Leadership
by Edgar H. Schein

Brave New
Work
by Aaron Dignan

The Fearless
Organization
by Amy Edmondson

[Mark]

I started junior high in the early '90s when public schools were getting rid of junk food and replacing it with healthy options. But none of the kids wanted healthy food. So one Halloween, I saved my candy, and after three weeks, I started selling it at school, each piece for a quarter. The next year I got smart. I saved up the money from doing odd jobs around the neighborhood and bought discounted candy the day after Halloween. This time I had so much candy that I was still selling it well into the spring. I roamed the halls with rolls of quarters in my pockets. Eventually, I got caught by a teacher who thought I was using the heavy rolls of quarters in fistfights. I'm still not sure how a scrappy eighth grader who headed the Star Trek Club got mistaken for a gangster throwing punches with rolls of quarters, but I took it as a badge of pride.

I graduated from selling fun-size candy bars to earning my marketing chops as a high school student working at Taco Bell. Ted moved on to his first real job working in a store selling music back when CDs were a new thing. Since those early days trying to earn a buck, both of us have seen how brand success has everything to do with what you do. In 2013, we partnered up and cofounded Historic Agency. The goal? To help organizations leverage culture, marketing, and design to drive results and build a brand crafted to endure.

Ted's a brilliant strategist who leads client transformation at Historic Agency. He specializes in executive leadership, brand development, marketing, and strategic clarity. He's worked for just about every type of organization—large and small, for-profit and nonprofit, healthy and toxic. He thrives most when he's helping leaders harness their organizational culture so they can do what they love and build a stand-out brand (he's also our resident foodie and sommelier).

I've spent the past two decades helping some of the fastest-growing and largest nonprofit organizations in the country develop brand and marketing strategies that fuel their mission to do more good. I studied film and video production, became a media director of a large nonprofit at the age of twenty, and went on to become a brand manager in the private sector. I've done client work, led in-house marketing teams, and helped rebrand organizations of all stripes. At Historic, I lead brand transformation and product design and strategy.

[Ted]

Historic Agency started out helping nonprofits accelerate their brand to make a greater impact. As we served these world-changing organizations, we saw how an aligned culture did more to grow communities of donors, volunteers, and advocates than anything else these nonprofits did. Their brand success began with culture.

We compared the experiences of our clients with our favorite consumer brands and started noticing patterns: top corporate brands such as REI and Apple do the same things our most effective nonprofits were doing. They build their brand from the inside out, starting with their culture. Their culture influences everything they do and aligns with the brand to ignite its success more than any amount of marketing ever could.

Since then, we've focused on helping organizations of every type leverage their culture to drive their brand. We stopped offering the standard single-sided solutions most marketing agencies sell because we knew that those tools and processes can't create long-term lift for the brand or sustain lasting results.

Instead, we designed the Marquee Culture method—a process that helps organizations transform their company culture so that it show-cases the brand and brings in more people. That's exactly what this book offers you: the know-how to create your own Marquee Culture that makes a huge promise, draws more customers, and gives your brand a competitive edge.

POSITIONING YOUR BRAND FOR CHANGE

The best brands can weather change and stay ahead of crises because their culture champions risk-taking and innovation. They aren't blindsided when storms come, and their employees have the agility to steer the brand through uncertainty.

In our rapidly changing society, your organization is only as successful as its ability to respond to the steady stream of challenges confronting your brand at a faster pace than ever. Having an aligned culture guides your people to innovate and courageously navigate change to win more customers and make your brand more profitable.

But it's not just about profits. We're willing to bet that you're driven by more than just the bottom line. You want to find meaning and purpose in what you do. And you want your organization to make a difference along the way. You envision a brand that goes beyond profits to do more good and positively influence your staff, your customers, and your community.

We wrote this book to help leaders like you build a brand that makes a difference—a brand that customers rave about. We distilled everything we've learned into a method to help you create an authentic brand with less spending on advertising. After reading this book, you'll have the tools you need to cultivate a culture that helps you and your team impact lives for the better.

So what are you waiting for?
Download your toolkit, and let's get started.

 culturebuiltmybrand.com/tools

CHAPTER 1

How Culture Eats Brand

What You'll Learn in This Chapter →

- how your culture poses the biggest barrier to growth and success—and what you can do to fix it

- how profitability and culture work hand in hand to win more customers

- why traditional solutions won't fix a broken culture or sustain lasting change

- how to build an authentic culture and spend less money on advertising

- how Netflix executives turned an epic leadership failure into a force that drives innovation

[Mark]

"Culture eats strategy for breakfast." These famous words are attributed to Peter Drucker, the late organizational management guru who observed how company culture can overpower the most effective business strategy. Almost every nonprofit and business leader I talk to knows this principle to be true. They've seen how their organizational culture can either support their strategy or tear it down. But what few leaders realize is that culture never gets full. Once it devours their strategy, it keeps going and eats through their entire brand.

The Invisible Brand Barrier

One of the first things I hear when we start working with a new client is "We have a brand problem." They can point to the visible issues: Their website isn't converting visitors into new leads. The customer experience is broken. They've got high employee turnover rates and shaky financial performance. Staff aren't performing as they should, and their marketing isn't driving traffic.

Leaders can see the surface problems, but it's harder to identify the underlying source of those problems. The real reason things aren't working is because of their culture—not their brand. Their problem is a misaligned culture that allows internal issues to undermine and erode brand success.

Culture is your organization's internal environment. It's made visible through how your team acts and makes decisions. "Culture is to a group what personality or character is to an individual," writes Edgar Schein in his book *Organizational Culture and Leadership*.[1] It produces shared behaviors and beliefs reflecting who you are as an organization. Culture dictates how you operate on the inside and shapes how your people behave according to what they believe to be acceptable within the group. How your organization operates internally, the decisions your people make, and how they act—these invisible aspects of your culture define your brand. That means your brand is only as successful and profitable as your culture allows it to be. When aligned with the brand to fuel results, culture becomes your secret power that differentiates your organization from the competition.

But most leaders don't know how to intentionally align their culture to their brand. At best, they create a culture independent of their brand

---

1   Edgar H. Schein, *Organizational Culture and Leadership*, 4th edition (San Francisco: Jossey-Bass, 2010), 14.

and miss out on opportunities to propel the organization's mission forward. At worst, leaders completely ignore their culture until it veers off-brand, creating internal problems that accelerate failure from the inside out.

In either case, disintegration between brand and culture is the biggest barrier to growth and financial success. A broken culture undermines everything it touches. It allows employees to perform off-brand or below expectations. It stagnates your marketing efforts, produces a lack of focus across the organization, and cripples the momentum your brand needs to drive forward.

Culture Fights Ugly

One client hired us to help them pivot their media strategy. Their market was changing rapidly, and their team needed to respond quickly to stay afloat. I pulled their core team into an interactive workshop modeled on design sprints, a tool that helps teams quickly align around a clearly defined strategy. The first goal was simple: to identify the team's most pressing challenges and prioritize which one to focus on first to get the biggest return.

The activity started great. Team members were engaged. Everyone offered good feedback. Then I handed them a bunch of pens and stacks of blank sticky notes. I gave them a few minutes to quietly write down all the challenges their organization faced. They dove into it (people really love writing on sticky notes).

Next, they needed to sort their sticky notes into groups and prioritize the problems. But when I asked them to share the challenges they'd written down, the room heated up. People started ranting about the

problems. With each new sticky note, team members listed all the reasons why that particular issue couldn't be solved:

- "There's not enough time."
- "I don't have the authority to make decisions and implement change."
- "We don't have the staff or budget."
- "I don't know what to prioritize."
- "I'm dependent on someone else for the information I need."

The workshop devolved into a screaming match as they vented over every problem, shot down each other's recommendations, and lobbed their excuses at each other. The exercise was simply meant to identify and prioritize the challenges. But team members couldn't get past their anger, arguing that each problem couldn't be fixed and there was nothing they could do about it.

How did this team get stuck here? They were victims of their organization's culture. Their protests pointed to issues with decision-making, access to resources, and power dynamics—all of which are driven by internal culture. Their biggest brand barrier was a culture eating away at their ability to push past broken policies and find real solutions to move their brand forward. They'd been held back by their culture and stewing on their frustration for so long that it finally bubbled up as paralysis and resentment.

Culture either aligns with a brand to sustain success or progressively overtakes the brand to devour it. A misaligned culture produces mediocre results, eats away at profit margins, and dismantles the brand strategy. The signs of disintegration are sometimes subtle. But they pose a serious threat to your brand's success. Here are some of the warning signs that point to a broken culture:

- Employees are quitting and you're struggling to retain new hires.

- Internal division has created factions and is crippling collaboration.

- Customer complaints show they're losing confidence and abandoning your brand.

- Your people are falling behind in performance and innovation.

- Team members seem incapable of embracing change for the sake of the brand.

- Decision-making often produces counterproductive strategies.

If you ignore problems such as these, you risk letting your brand be commandeered by a culture that blocks success.

Why Solving for Symptoms Misses the Problem

Leaders often turn to more traditional solutions to solve problems caused by misalignment of brand and culture. Instead of digging deep to the root cause, they pursue quick fixes: They rewrite their values or hire an agency to design a sophisticated digital marketing campaign. Sometimes they try offering more employee perks. Those solutions may bring about some improvements. But the changes are short-lived. Soon enough, the culture pushes the same problems back to the surface, no matter how much work went into trying to eliminate them.

Another nonprofit client came to us when it was bleeding donors and losing money. Executives had pursued a number of solutions. They just didn't know how to find the right solutions. Instead, they had hired a fundraiser who overpromised and underdelivered and dumped

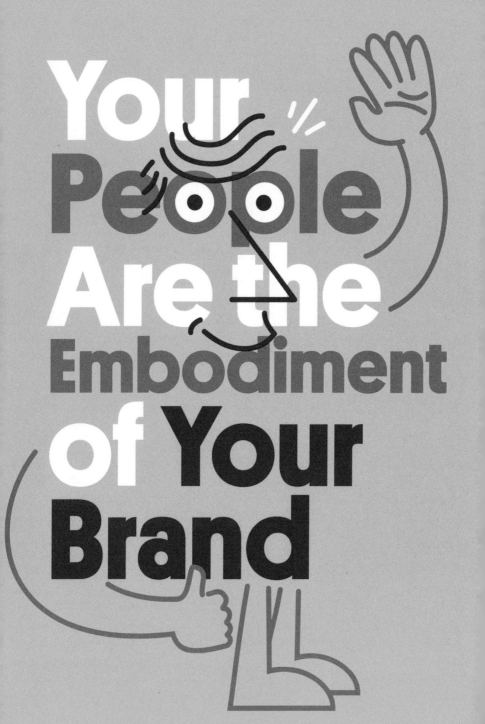

Your People Are the Embodiment of Your Brand

hundreds of thousands of dollars into ineffective marketing. Those failed solutions multiplied their losses and put them in a worse situation.

What these executives didn't recognize was the depth of their disintegration. The nonprofit had a powerful set of ideals guiding its internal culture, and its employees had embraced these ideals and bought into the mission wholeheartedly. But the organization hadn't applied those values to the donor experience. That meant its audience wasn't experiencing what the brand promised.

We infused the nonprofit's values into its donor communications, and we helped create powerful touchpoints allowing its external audiences to experience firsthand what the brand stood for. Executives and their teams aligned their day-to-day operations so that everything they did naturally communicated the brand and supported its promise.

It worked. As they aligned their culture with the brand, the executives saw a nearly immediate difference. Donors started experiencing more authentically and consistently what the organization offered as employees began to live out the brand in all of their interactions. This regained donors' trust and ultimately did the heavy lifting of marketing, which meant the nonprofit could spend less on advertising to gain and retain donors. That first year, the organization soared past its fundraising goals. During the next year, it nearly doubled its donor base, and it received its first seven-figure gift, a donation from someone who had just been waiting for a brand that was authentic to its promise and proved worthy of investment.

Building a Brand That Awakens Your Audience

When Ted and I founded Historic, we started out with a focus on helping nonprofits make a bigger impact. Nonprofits don't sell products to their audience. They sell purpose. The most successful nonprofits awaken their audience to a cause worth investing in and help people feel like they are making a difference. That doesn't happen if all the organization has is a nice-looking website and logo. Brands succeed by infusing the promise of purpose into every layer of their internal culture so that it reaches their audience and wins more customers.

Any marketing agency worth its salt can design a beautiful website, a stunning logo, and an engaging advertising campaign. But these one-time efforts don't create big lift for your brand. To awaken your audience to your purpose, you need the strength of an internally aligned culture that helps your people showcase your brand, shapes how they operate on the inside, and powers results on the outside.

A Culture That Guides Your People

Let's look at your most important asset: your employees. Your people are the embodiment of your brand. When they're engaged and motivated, they produce results that are meaningful, consistent, and innovative. But when their daily decisions and actions are at odds with your brand, you begin to see problems that trickle down to adversely affect product delivery. Customer experiences don't line up with what you've promised them, and your followers eventually abandon your brand for one that's more authentic.

Your brand isn't what you say it is. It's what you do. That's where culture comes into play. Culture deeply influences what you do—how your employees behave and make decisions. Your brand may promise excellent customer service, but if your culture incentivizes employees to hit sales targets instead of rewarding them for adding value to people's lives, then you'll fail to delight customers. Your audience will lose trust and stop buying into what you say about your brand. You can't blame your employees for focusing on the rewarded behavior. They're simply guided by your internal culture—not by what you say about your brand.

Culture isn't good or bad. It exists whether you want it to or not. The question is whether you'll let it evolve on its own and become your biggest liability—or intentionally harness it to empower your people to deliver on your brand promise.

Why Culture Is Ignored

If I talk about organizational health, most leaders get it. Thanks to the work of leadership experts like Patrick Lencioni, author of *The Five Dysfunctions of a Team,* most executives know how to recognize when their organizational health is good or bad. But rarely do they ask whether that health is on- or off-brand.

Your business or nonprofit may be organizationally healthy. It could be a place of high empathy, vulnerability, and goodwill. But having a healthy organization isn't enough to build a successful brand. Health is the minimum standard. Your organizational health needs to go further. It needs to be on-brand. It doesn't matter how healthy your organization is if it's not helping people execute your brand's purpose.

The Hidden Stabilizers of On-Brand Health

On-brand organizational health is built on the dual foundations of clarity and trust. Without clarity and trust, organizations generally struggle to maintain long-term success.

CLARITY

Executives often hold an intuitive understanding of the mission, values, and vision driving their brand. But that clear understanding rarely gets transferred to employees. When there's no clarity around the mission and purpose, there's almost always a lack of clarity around the key metrics defining your brand's success.

We worked with one nonprofit whose mission it was to bring about social change for hundreds of millions of people across the globe. But executives couldn't define how they measured success. In fact, they were resistant to the idea of defining brand impact.

The nonprofit appeared to be a healthy organization, and its staff were among the kindest, most courageous people in the world. But their internal teams were working at cross purposes. Without a shared understanding of what on-brand success looked like, employees had no reason to align their efforts. That missing clarity kept the nonprofit from making a greater difference in the world.

If you don't clarify the metrics that define brand success, you allow your employees to drift and lose focus, often resulting in competing agendas and self-serving silos. This cripples your organization with counterproductive strategies, wasted resources, and sideways energy.

Here's how to build clarity in your organization: infuse your brand into everything you do. Elevate your mission and purpose so that it shapes your people's behavior and informs the decisions they make. I know that's easier said than done. But as you work through this book, the pieces will come together. You'll have greater clarity guiding your people to make huge contributions toward your brand's success.

TRUST

For your employees to do great work, they need to trust that it's safe to fail when they take a well-calculated risk for the brand. Without trust, teams produce work far below their capacity and skill. Lack of trust kills creativity, fosters fear, and leads to high turnover.

Trust has two sides: relational and functional. Relational trust is rooted in feelings. It builds empathy, vulnerability, and a sense of safety. The overriding question with relational trust is, "Do you understand me and want the best for me?"

Functional Trust
Relational Trust

Relational

Resides in the heart & is more rooted in feeling. Built on behaviors like:

Empathy · Vulnerability
Forgiveness · Familiarity
Goodwill

Functional

Resides in the head & is more rooted in thinking. Built on behaviors like:

Performance · Consistency
Accuracy · Delivery
Communication

Functional trust is based on logic, performance, consistency, and delivery. It asks, "Did you do what you're supposed to do?" Functional trust requires an organization-wide understanding of success so that employees are held accountable to the mission.

When these two types of trust are in balance, the result is amazing productivity that breeds inspiration, creativity, and innovation across the organization. But most organizations tend to favor one type of trust over the other. For instance, nonprofits are typically marked by high relational trust because of the missional dimension of their work. Employees feel a strong commitment to the cause and a sense of loyalty to the brand purpose. But leaders in these organizations often find it difficult to define success and build systems of accountability. Their functional trust lags behind as well-meaning and passionate staff are allowed to slip on results or expectations. Where functional trust asks, "Did you do what you're supposed to do?" employees in these organizations answer with some version of, "No, but I really do care!"

Organizations that favor functional trust tend to operate with clear systems of accountability and performance management. Employees who fail to measure up usually don't last long. But teams in these organizations often struggle with empathy and goodwill. The answer to the relational question of, "Do you understand me?" may sound like, "No, and that doesn't matter because you screwed up."

To build healthy, high-performing teams that work together to advance the brand, you need both relational and functional trust. This balance of trust results in teams that can take creative risks—and even fail—while driving the brand toward its ultimate goal.

We talk about trust throughout this book because we've seen how critical it is to brand success. Here's the good news: as you align your culture with your brand, it has an organic balancing effect on trust. It strengthens both functional trust and relational trust, leading to employees who are more engaged, perform better, and turn into brilliant brand advocates.

Optimizing Trust and Clarity to Sustain Your Brand

Trust and clarity work together to stabilize organizational health and sustain brand success. Without trust and clarity, your team won't know what it looks like to perform on-brand, and they won't develop the confidence to innovate or take bold risks.

Broken brands can appear to be healthy, even as they lose momentum and hit performance barriers. Coworkers may get along with each other and feel invested in the organization. But without a clear and common bull's-eye for success, they don't know how their work contributes to the bottom line, or worse, what the bottom line even is. If that lack of clarity doesn't get addressed, it will eventually build frustration and erode trust—because when employees don't know if they're succeeding, their sense of contribution and satisfaction quickly deteriorates.

Other organizations may have amazing clarity around their mission, values, and key performance indicators but lack a culture of empathy and trust. Employees have a ruthlessly clear understanding of success, but they don't feel a sense of connection or investment. They tend to compete, create silos, and develop turf-protection strategies instead of collaborating in trust-filled partnerships that push the brand past performance barriers.

You need both clarity and trust to build a culture that supports your vision and purpose. That means going beyond organizational health to make sure that your employees not only experience trusting relationships, but also work toward the same brand outcomes. Organizational health can't be an end in itself. Ted and I didn't write this book so you could learn how to make your organization healthy. We wrote it to equip you to understand and invest in your culture so you can build a stand-out brand that gets better results. Organizational health is simply a means to that end. Great brands don't aim for health as an end goal. They go beyond and optimize it by aligning it with the brand to create a compelling, consistent promise.

How Your Leadership Shapes Your Culture

As a leader, you shape your culture by what you say and do. It doesn't matter if you're intentional about it or not. The more senior your position, the more impact you have on your culture. The question is whether the culture you're reinforcing is the culture your brand needs to stand out. If you fail to shape the right culture, it can completely derail the brand and—as in one major brand's case—cost millions of dollars.

THE QUICK-LIVED QWIKSTER

Netflix CEO and cofounder Reed Hastings experienced huge successes in the start-up's early days. He helped shape the high-achieving culture that allowed the company to outpace major competitors and go on to lead the media and tech industry.

In 2007, Netflix started offering free streaming on top of its DVD-by-mail subscription service. Within a few years, the company had more than twenty million subscribers streaming videos online, and Hastings saw an opportunity to turn Netflix into the number one streaming company. In 2011, he announced that the company was dismantling its old subscription package that had offered DVDs and unlimited streaming for $10 a month. The basic service would be replaced with two separate services, one for streaming and one for DVD-by-mail, the latter of which they renamed Qwikster. Each service would cost about $8 a month.

None of this went over well with customers. Netflix subscribers blasted the company for turning a simple service into a more expensive package with a terrible name. About 800,000 customers canceled their subscription, and Netflix's stock plummeted by 70 percent.[2]

Before Hasting's plan went into effect, many of Netflix's senior executives had reservations about it. But instead of telling Hastings that his idea was a mistake, they kept quiet. Maybe they were afraid to speak up. Maybe they didn't want to express doubt in Hastings, who had been right about almost every other major decision up to now. Regardless, their silence was nearly fatal to the company.

As Qwikster backfired, Hastings admitted that his plan had been misguided, and his senior team learned a costly lesson about bringing doubts to the table before launching new ideas. In response, they created an internal process that encourages employees to submit their ideas to peer scrutiny. In a practice they call "farming for dissent," employees pitch their proposals in an open Google Docs file. Others write down whether they think the idea is wise or just plain stupid. This process gives team members a chance to speak up and point out what's wrong with an idea while it's still in its early stages.

Qwikster exposed Netflix's culture at the time—a culture Hastings had unintentionally created. If left unchecked, that culture would have allowed top leaders to keep making bad decisions that deteriorated the brand. Instead, Hastings and his team pivoted by developing a process to stop employees from deferring to the people in charge and equip them to challenge ideas. Since then, Netflix has far outpaced the competition in innovation and customer satisfaction.

Reinforcing Culture

As a leader, you can either intentionally build a culture that supports your brand—or single-handedly derail it. Good leadership requires constant

---

2 "Netflix Is a Team, Not a Family," June 23, 2020, in *Land of the Giants*, produced by Vox, podcast, Apple Podcasts, https://podcasts.apple.com/us/podcast/netflix-is-a-team-not-a-family/id1465767420?i=1000479218645.

attention. Culture isn't "a 'set it and forget it' endeavor," writes author and venture capitalist Ben Horowitz. "You must constantly examine and reshape your culture or it won't be your culture at all."[3] Your approach to culture needs to be proactive. That means reinforcing it daily.

It's hard to be intentional about cultivating the right culture. I know what it's like to have so many spinning plates to juggle and fires to put out. With everything clamoring for your attention, it's easy to push culture to the wayside and let it evolve on its own. But when you do that, you miss out on the opportunity to leverage your culture to build the brand you want. At the end of the day, you have to make time for your culture. Your organization's success depends on it.

The Key to Better Marketing with Less Spend

Consumer brands such as Netflix don't depend on advertising to generate revenue. Just like our most successful clients at Historic, the best brands of our time create a culture that does the hard work of marketing for them. They integrate their brand into every layer of culture—from their core values down to the distinct words they use— to support their employees as they create purpose and value for their audience. Their culture shapes every decision and filters down to turn consumers into brand evangelists. It sets up their people to deliver consistently on their brand promise to create bigger lift with less spend.

Whether you're a nonprofit leader or a business executive, it's up to you to shape your culture so that it supports your people to fulfill your brand promise. You can choose to ignore your culture and let it evolve on its own—until it devours everything you've worked for. Or you can harness the power of culture to push your brand past the barriers that have been holding it back.

---

3   Ben Horowitz, *What You Do Is Who You Are: How to Create Your Business Culture* (New York: Harper Collins, 2019), 122.

In the next chapter, Ted rolls out the blueprint for brand and culture alignment. He explains each of the pillars that support your brand. He also gets into the bread and butter of keeping your brand promise—and why every small decision matters when it comes to leveraging your culture to build a stand-out brand.

Your Key Takeaways

- The problems you see in your organization usually point to an invisible culture that's out of alignment with your brand.

- The driving force behind your brand's momentum is your internal culture—not your external identity or marketing strategy. When you infuse your brand into your culture, it accelerates results and becomes your greatest driver of success.

- Brand and culture alignment supports your staff to become advocates whose decisions and actions inspire customers to do the heavy lifting of marketing for you.

- Organizational health isn't an end in itself. It should align with the brand and be anchored in trust and clarity to help your team do consistently great work and outperform the competition.

- As a senior leader, you shape your culture—even when you're not aware of it. Integrating your brand into your culture takes constant reinforcement, but it pays off with engaged employees, loyal customers, and sustained success.

CHAPTER 2

Are You Keeping Your Promise?

What You'll Learn in
This Chapter ⟶

- how misalignment can compromise your brand and derail your strategy

- how to prevent your team from pursuing projects that do irreparable damage to the brand

- how to customize your approach to brand and culture alignment

- how to lay a foundation to build a culture that turns employees into brilliant brand ambassadors

- why it matters whether you stock your office kitchen with LaCroix or Dr. Pepper

[Ted]

I'm what you might call a foodie. I love going to new restaurants. I love cooking, studying wine, and digging into the finer details of global cuisine.

So when a top-tier restaurant in my neighborhood announced that a hot new chef from Los Angeles would be taking over its kitchen, I was more excited than most. I had eaten at the local restaurant before, and I was well aware of the owner's fastidious commitment to all things foodie: local produce, sustainably harvested seafood, bold and complex flavors, and a fantastic wine program.

Months ahead of the chef's debut, the restaurant got its brand and marketing strategy firing on all cylinders. The food press featured compelling interviews with the owner and new chef. The upcoming menu seemed inspired. Virtual sneak peeks into the refurbished restaurant showed bright, airy spaces featuring French modern art and pastel tones with bronze accents. Everything about the restaurant promised, "This will be incredible!"

I booked a reservation during the chef's debut month. When the day finally came, I discovered that everything was indeed incredible—except for one thing: the food. The flavors were muted and the textures odd. Salt was lacking. And the famous bread they used to bake in-house and serve with Normandy butter—once a restaurant staple—had been replaced with cheap substitutes.

This is what brand and culture misalignment feels like: to be let down by a brand that makes a big promise and then fails to carry it out. When a brand's promise doesn't match what it actually delivers, customers are left with the sour taste of disappointment. And when this happens consistently, the brand loses its credibility, its customers, and its market position.

The 5 Pillars of Brand

Many people think that brand is simply a matter of having a logo and a website. But you don't have a brand. You are a brand.

Visible elements are undoubtedly critical to your brand. But they comprise only one part of it. Your brand is much more comprehensive. It's the collective sum of everything you and your people say and do. It includes how your leaders make decisions, the way your audience feels about your brand, the comments people make online and off, and the story you communicate to the world.

We refer to brand as the sum of five parts:

- **Culture:** who you are—the convictions driving your mission, the values holding your organization together, and the behaviors defining your brand
- **Story:** what you say—the marketing narrative communicating who you are to your audience; the explicit articulation of your brand, its mission, and its values
- **Service/Product:** what you do—simply put, the product you sell or the service you provide
- **Experience:** how you feel—the physical or digital touchpoints you offer; how your people feel about their experience, which determines whether they'll keep engaging
- **Identity:** how you look—the aesthetic qualities of your brand that your audience sees first; your logo, website, visual identity, and design

These five pillars combine to create your brand promise. They tell your audience what to expect from your brand regardless of the channel or medium they use to connect with you. You build trust with your audience by making a promise and delivering on it with consistency. That trust retains customers, builds brand believers, and creates advocates who generate more awareness and buzz for your brand than any traditional marketing strategy ever could.

Outdated marketing tends to focus exclusively on the pillar of identity. It invests in advertising, websites, and social media while neglecting the other dimensions of brand. But out of all five pillars, culture most determines and sustains success. Culture cascades into everything you do. Like glue binding your brand together, it frames the other pillars into alignment and stabilizes them into a single entity that makes an authentic promise consistent with what your brand is actually about.

How Misalignment Compromises Your Brand Promise

Your brand isn't what you say it is. It's what you do. It's the outcome of your employees' daily decisions and behaviors, which are guided by your internal culture. The actions of your people add up to create experiences that either align to deliver on what you say you offer or mount up to diminish it.

When your brand and culture don't line up, your organization struggles to carry out your brand promise. This inevitably reaches customers in the form of brand gaps—the misalignment between what your brand says it offers and what your internal culture truly supports your people to deliver. The wider the gaps between what you say you do and what you actually deliver, the more you lose credibility and engagement with your audience. If your people aren't set up to execute on a convincing and compelling promise as they go about their daily activities, then your marketing attempts will only expose brand gaps and accelerate failure.

Mark and I have helped several businesses and nonprofits recover their brand after they paid buckets of money to someone who built them a misaligned identity. Typically these organizations ended up receiving a stunning logo and an impressive website, but these visual elements didn't match how they operated or what they delivered. Eventually, leaders realized they had bigger problems on their hands: a promise their brand couldn't execute, which widened the brand gaps and caused customers to lose confidence.

On the other end of the spectrum, we've seen world-changing brands with such a broken sense of identity that it prevents them from connecting with their market.

Culture's Impact on Brand Strategy

One of our nonprofit clients sought to tackle some of the most pressing global challenges around the world. They had an amazing strategy that had already empowered communities and strengthened entire nations. Recognizing the power of their approach to bring about desperately needed transformation across the globe, the nonprofit's senior executives started dreaming big. They drew up a strategy to partner with other organizations and expand the scope of their work to reach more communities in more countries.

But their broken identity blocked them from getting the traction they needed to attract potential partners and donors. Their dated visuals failed to articulate who they were, and their story was muddled and confusing. The language they used to describe their work was peppered with bloated and complicated phrases that impaired staff's ability to speak clearly about the organization's successes. Because it was so difficult to describe their work, employees simply stopped sharing the incredible accounts of the nonprofit's impact. Their story and identity were so out of sync, they held back the brand's momentum.

Mark and I walked them through the Marquee Culture method to align their brand and culture. We helped them refine their lexicon and clarify their story. Employees learned to talk about brand impact in ways that resonated with their audience. Together we created experiences for donors and partners to join in celebrating on-brand accomplishments. Layer by layer, we strengthened their internal culture to help their team live out the brand in their day-to-day operations. Today, the nonprofit is a global brand with a fresh visual identity showcasing who they are with authenticity and clarity. Through its expanded international network, our client now partners with dozens of nonprofit, private, and governmental organizations to make a greater difference around the world.

The most successful organizations create a clear and compelling brand promise that rings true to their audience, draws people in, and turns customers into loyal advocates. They align their culture to showcase their brand and deliver on that promise. At the same time, this alignment prevents them from wasting resources on single-sided strategies and brand-crippling decision-making.

How Culture Contributed to JCPenney's Demise

Corporate executive Ron Johnson had a lot going for him when he took the helm as JCPenney's new CEO in 2011. Years earlier he'd been an executive at Target and helped create the brand's iconic cheap-chic identity.[4] After that, he became the senior vice president of retail operations at Apple, where he spearheaded the Genius Bar, a signature retail feature that Steve Jobs originally labeled as idiotic.[5]

When Johnson stepped in as CEO, JCPenney was struggling and its revenue was in steady decline. Convinced he could transform the company into the next Apple, Johnson set about creating a new kind of retail experience, redesigning stores into collectives of trendsetting boutiques.

But the people who shopped at JCPenney didn't care how trendy the stores looked. They cared about saving money. Shopping for deals on deeply discounted clearance racks gave them a powerful sense of value. But Johnson didn't test his ideas to find out whether customers would buy into the new JCPenney. He went ahead with eliminating the constant markdowns and coupons that drove the company's

---

4   Andria Cheng, "Ron Johnson Made Apple Stores the Envy of Retail and Target Hip, But This Startup May Be His Crowning Achievement," *Forbes*, January 17, 2020, https://www.forbes.com/sites/andriacheng/2020/01/17/he-made-apple-stores-envy-of-retail-and-target-hip-but-his-biggest--career-chapter-may-be-just-starting.

5   Aric Jenkins, "Steve Jobs Thought the Apple Store Genius Bars Was 'So Idiotic' at First," *Fortune*, March 7, 2017, https://fortune.com/2017/03/07/steve-jobs-genius-bar-apple-store.

sales. He instituted a fair-and-square pricing structure, essentially dismantling the business strategy JCPenney had relied on for years. The response? Customers ditched their loyalty and abandoned the brand. Less than a year and a half after taking the job, Johnson was fired. As I write, JCPenney's future remains precarious. In 2020, the company filed for bankruptcy, shuttered more than 170 stores, closed its corporate headquarters, fired its CEO, and was sold to new owners.[6]

The difference between Johnson's destructive tenure at JCPenney and his success at Apple comes down to one simple matter: culture. At Apple, Johnson benefited from a culture infused with the brand at every level. That alignment kept Johnson from veering off track with decisions that could derail Apple's brand promise. Meanwhile, JCPenney's brand was already disintegrating by the time Johnson came on the scene. Without an aligned culture to keep the new executive on-brand, he was able to set a course marked by unchecked decisions, to devastating effect.

Every Decision Matters

Each decision counts—not only the big, strategic decisions, but also the seemingly insignificant ones. Consider all the little choices that have to be made in your organization every single day. For better or worse, the decisions your people make and the ways they behave shape your culture and reveal your values. Remember that you have a culture whether you're intentional about it or not.

Take workplace snacks as an example. Whether you provide free food for your staff communicates something about your culture. So do the types of snacks you offer. You can be like Mark and try stocking your

---

6   Michael Lisicky, "JCPenney, Under New Ownership, Is Homeless for the Holidays," *Forbes*, December 12, 2020, https://www.forbes.com/sites/michaellisicky/2020/12/12/jcpenney-under-new-ownership-is-homeless-for-the-holidays.

office kitchen with Red Vines and Dr. Pepper—just as long as you don't mind your team's productivity tanking after their sugar high wears off. Or you can provide healthy food, sparkling water, and protein snacks. You can offer no food at all, and then your employees leave the office to buy snacks off-site.

Decisions like these are neither right nor wrong. They simply reflect your internal culture. They help reveal what's important in your organization and shape how your people act as they deliver on your promise. Having a Marquee Culture ensures that any employee at any level of your organization is equipped to make the decisions that support your brand.

Aligning Culture with Brand

Early on, Mark and I discovered that culture was the last thing many of our clients wanted to invest in. They often ignored culture and let it evolve on its own. We noticed a pattern with these types of clients: every rebrand we rolled out for them got rejected. It didn't matter how much the client loved the name, logo, and visual assets we had designed for them. At the end of the day, the culture simply ate the work we did. Within a year or so, each of these organizations would go back to the way things were before the rebrand. In the most extreme cases, clients went as far as killing their new websites and firing the executive who had led the rebranding initiative.

These experiences quickly taught us that we needed to address culture at the same time we addressed brand because if our clients continued ignoring culture, it would affect their bottom line, rob them of customers, and disintegrate their mission and purpose. So instead of offering the traditional one-sided rebranding solutions, we started designing processes to help organizations examine and shape their culture. We built customizable tools to help them find their unique approach to aligning culture and brand. As a result, our clients have sustained brilliant results long after they've moved on from us.

There is no one-size-fits-all approach to integrating your brand into the layers of your culture. Your organization deserves a process tailored to draw out its unique culture to support your success. Alignment takes hard work, ruthless honesty, and a tireless commitment to holding fast to your promise. But it doesn't take a miracle. Creating a great brand begins simply by building a foundational understanding of who you are and the promise you make to your customers.

How to Build a Brilliant Brand

The first step of brand and culture alignment is to develop a comprehensive understanding of your brand. To help our clients do that well, we take them through the BrandMaker process. The BrandMaker is a robust, practical tool we designed to systematically outline each brand pillar—culture, story, service or product, experience, and identity. It looks at everything inside a brand and ensures it's all pointing toward your promise.

Our process goes deeper than other brand tools that help organizations refine their messaging. It will move you further by helping you integrate every dimension of your brand into the greater whole—because no matter how hard you've worked on your messaging, if the rest of your brand doesn't line up to support it, you'll still fail to deliver on expectations. The BrandMaker is especially helpful for complex organizations with multiple teams, different services, and diverse sets of clients that each require unique messaging. It ensures that every element remains on-brand.

We recommend that you gather your leadership team and walk through the BrandMaker tool, available in full at culturebuiltmybrand.com/tools. It will help you conceptualize and clarify your brand and give you a stable foundation for cultivating an integrated internal culture that makes your brand stand out.

A Culture That Showcases Brand

Your culture is loud. Every culture is. It's meant to be the loudest expression of your brand. Your culture determines how your employees act, the decisions they make, and the quality of their work. Your employees, in turn, broadcast your brand and can provide the customer experience that remains true to your promise. When your internal culture is aligned with the promise you make on the outside, it drives your success more than any other dimension of your brand.

Many executives stop listening to their own culture and miss the very thing that screams to others. But leaders of great organizations stay attuned to their culture and infuse their brand into every aspect of their employees' day-to-day reality. That's what the Marquee Culture method is all about. A Marquee Culture is like a brightly lit sign that announces what your brand stands for. It showcases who you are, what you do, and what customers can expect from you. By aligning each layer of your culture with the brand, you make a big promise and help your people live it out in everything they do. It turns your employees into advocates who create such a radiant brand that you end up spending less on advertising. A Marquee Culture is brand strategy from the inside out.

Building a Marquee Culture is equal parts art and science. We lay out the science in the following chapters with a systematic, practical method that infuses each layer of your culture with your brand. This creates an irresistible employee experience that engages your team to produce sensational work and more innovative results. And that's where the artistry comes in. A Marquee Culture sets up your people to carry your brand further than you ever imagined.

The Six Layers of Culture That Drive Results

In the next six chapters, we take you through each step of the Marquee Culture method. You'll dive into the layers of your culture and gain the tools you need to chart a course for brand and culture alignment. We use real-world examples and insights from everyday businesses and big consumer brands to show how organizations of every type and size can tap into their culture to gain a competitive advantage. Near the end of every chapter, we outline the practical steps to engage your employees and build customer loyalty.

We start in chapter 3 with Principles, the immovable values that comprise the first foundational layer of your culture. This chapter shows you how to connect your core values to specific employee behaviors that make your brand stand out.

Chapter 4 is about your Architecture—the internal systems and structures that, when designed to reflect your brand, support your staff to deliver consistently on your promise and turn customers into loyal fans.

The final four chapters walk you through each consecutive layer of culture: Rituals, Lore, Vocabulary, and Artifacts. When intentionally crafted, these layers build upon each other to create a Marquee Culture that reinforces the brand for the staff who drive it forward.

How They Do It

At the end of each chapter, we provide brief real-world analysis of how three of our favorite companies have operationalized their brands into everything they do. These are small everyday organizations led by passionate people who have aligned their culture with their brand to produce outstanding results. Here's a chance to get to know them before we move ahead.

CLARK | CLARK.IS

Clark is a B2B company specializing in audio, visual, and lighting systems and production design. With clients ranging from houses of worship to theme parks and cruise lines, the Clark team pursues excellence and innovation while creating the best solutions at the lowest cost. Its mission is to deliver world-class production systems that are scaled to save clients time and money.

- Year founded: 1995
- Based in: Atlanta, GA
- Size: over fifty full-time employees and five locations across the US

MONIKER GROUP | MONIKERGROUP.COM

Moniker Group empowers talented creatives to use their gifts and build companies that matter. What started out as a design fabrication studio has launched into a collective of companies that includes a coworking space, retail store, coffee shop, cocktail bar, multiple event venues, and catering. Moniker exists to cultivate community, create spaces, and invest in others as they move toward their dreams.

- Year founded: 2010
- Based in: San Diego, CA
- Size: over fifty employees and eight businesses located across San Diego

NICO'S BARBER SHOP | NICOSBARBERSHOP.COM

Known for great haircuts, exceptional service, and attention to detail, Nico's is a full-service barbershop that creates impact over profit. "Look good, do good" inspires how they operate, and it engages customers with its mission to make a positive difference in the community. Nico's recently launched its own product line and is gearing up to expand with a new location in Phoenix.

- Year founded: 2018
- Based in: Gilbert, AZ
- Size: over twelve employees, two Arizona locations, and growing

Harnessing Your Culture to Build a Stand-Out Brand

Mark and I know firsthand that aligning your organization takes focus and work. You'll have to be willing to scrutinize everything you do. Some of the challenges you'll face along the way will be painful and require brutal honesty about what matters most to your organization. Plenty of leaders aren't willing to do the work, and they wind up with a brand that lags behind and struggles to gain a profitable share of the market.

Don't let that be you. We'll help you harness your culture so that your brand stays ahead of the pack. Going forward, you'll need courage and grit, but the potential payoff in increased employee engagement, customer loyalty, and momentum is well worth the effort.

Next up is Principles, the foundational layer of your culture. Onward!

THE BRANDMAKER PROCESS
Kick-Start Alignment by Clarifying Your Brand

The BrandMaker is a tool we designed to help you go deep into each pillar of your brand. As you work through this process, you'll develop a comprehensive understanding of your brand and ensure that it lines up with the greater whole. Consider working through the BrandMaker, found at culturebuiltmybrand.com/tools, with your leadership team. When you're done, you'll have a more robust understanding and appreciation of your brand so you can start integrating it into everything you do using the Marquee Culture method.

Your Key Takeaways

- You don't have a brand. You are a brand.

- Your brand is the collective sum of everything your organization believes, says, and does. The comments you post on social media, the care you extend to your community, the remarks customers make about their experience—these all shape your brand.

- Culture is just one pillar of your brand; however, it's the dimension that most determines and sustains results. No matter how much you spend on your visual identity, it's all wasted if you don't invest in your culture.

- As your people live out your brand, they deliver on your brand promise and build loyalty and trust with your audience.

- Building a Marquee Culture isn't easy, but it will fuel success from the inside out and turn customers into loyal advocates.

PRINCIPLES

CHAPTER 3

Principles

Actions Speak Louder than Words

PRINCIPLES:

Behavior-based values that guide your people to act, behave, and make decisions that reflect the brand and bring it to life

What You'll Learn in This Chapter ⟶

- why values do so little for your brand and how to fix it

- how behavior-based Principles inspire your people to do great work and showcase your brand at its best

- how to model, promote, and reward the behaviors and decisions that win more customers

- what brands can learn from do-what-I-say parenting

[Ted]

I grew up hearing "Do what I say, not what I do" from my parents (all four of them). To be honest, I'm guilty of parenting that way, too. Just like my girls today, I wasn't aware or able, then, to say how important it was for me to see consistency between my parents' actions and words. I couldn't articulate how that lack of consistency created trust gaps and hindered my ability to be influenced by my parents.

This is often the starting place for cultural breakdown. If key leaders are unclear as to how the brand they serve informs their actions and behaviors, they will fail to model those critical behaviors and culture will not scale.

[Mark & Ted]

Guiding values. Core virtues. Distinctives. Whatever you call them, most organizations have a list of values they hope will define the brand and drive meaningful difference.

Leaders tend to view their organizational values as sacrosanct. But in misaligned organizations, those values are often ambiguous and lofty. They hold little meaning for employees and don't show people how to perform to deliver on-brand outcomes. Without a clear picture of how their behaviors support the brand, employees end up performing in ways that undermine it.

Your people don't need aspirational values that point to abstract outcomes. They need Principles modeled by their leaders and tied to everyday behaviors that reflect the brand and support its success.

Principles over Values

Values usually come from the top of an organization. A senior leader presents a list of values to executives and board members. Everyone shakes hands on it. But then nothing in the organization changes. Simply articulating organizational values doesn't help employees live them out. They keep functioning just as they did before. Daily operations, performance outcomes, and the customer experience all stay the same—or worse, they deteriorate.

All too often, leaders phrase their values as vague, aspirational beliefs that do little to shape the culture they need. Rarely do they operationalize these values into tangible actions. As a result, few employees understand how to turn their day-to-day decisions and behaviors into actions that support the brand.

Only
27%
of employees strongly believe in their organizations' values.

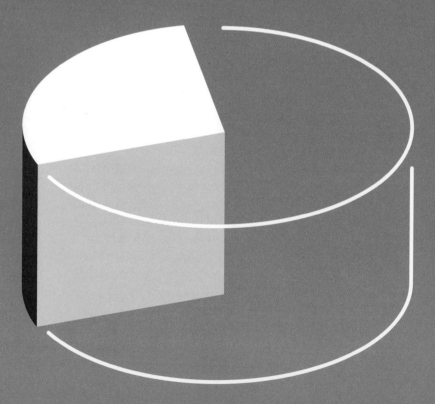

Principles, however, are based on behavior, not belief. They show people what it looks like to perform to organizational standards, interact with others, and deliver on the brand promise. At the end of the day, employees need behavior-based Principles that give them a crystal-clear understanding of how to behave to elevate the brand and differentiate it from the competition.

THE FORGETTABLE NATURE OF VALUES

Most employees go about their day-to-day work with little awareness of their organization's values. According to a Gallup study, fewer than half of employees in the US strongly agree that they know what their organization stands for and what differentiates it from the competition.[7] Only 27 percent strongly believe in their organization's values.[8] Even fewer strongly agree that they can apply their organization's values to their everyday work.[9]

But executives still rely on ambiguous corporate values to guide their employees' performance. When their staff fail to demonstrate those values, leaders tend to blame it on seemingly indifferent employees. The real problem is that leaders haven't tied their values to specific, actionable behaviors. They've failed to give employees a clear picture of how those values get played out in their day-to-day work. Cultivating behaviors that guide on-brand performance requires going beyond values and equipping your employees to truly live out what your brand stands for.

---

7   Adam Hickman, "Check Your Culture: 3 Questions for Managers," *Gallup*, September 13, 2019, https://www.gallup.com/workplace/266702/check-culture-questions-managers.aspx.

8   Nate Dvorak and Bailey Nelson, "Few Employees Believe in Their Company's Values," *Gallup*, September 13, 2016, https://news.gallup.com/businessjournal/195491/few-employees-believe-company-values.aspx.

9   Ibid.

WORDS ON A WALL

With everything clamoring for your attention as a leader, it can be tempting to throw out empty words such as "integrity" and "quality," hoping they come to define your brand. But treating your set of values as a vague afterthought leads to an underperforming brand at best or a series of Enron-scale lawsuits at worst.

In 2002, Enron was listed as America's fifth-largest company.[10] Meanwhile, the energy trading corporation was engaged in one of the biggest accounting frauds in history. Leaders cooked the books and pocketed millions of dollars. Over a dozen former executives went to prison for conspiracy, fraud, and insider trading.

Before the company's epic downfall, Enron's four core values—including integrity—were plastered on the wall of its lobby. But this prominent visibility didn't transfer to how Enron leadership behaved and made decisions. Either the values were not integrated into their culture or the staff just considered them meaningless words on the wall. In the absence of clearly defined behaviors that reflected the brand, Enron fostered a disintegrated culture that allowed people to defy its values, behave badly, and be rewarded for it.

Great brands go beyond values by operationalizing them into their employees' daily decisions and behaviors. They exchange easily forgotten words for practical, actionable ways to live out the brand. They bring their values to life and make them visible through distinctive behaviors that drive on-brand results.

---

10 "A Database of 50 Years of Fortune's List of America's Largest Corporations," *Fortune*, accessed November 15, 2020, https://archive.fortune.com/magazines/fortune/fortune500_archive/full/2002.

Actions Speak Louder than Marketing

Your best marketing strategy is your people. Every employee at every level of your organization is a brand ambassador. Their decisions, no matter how big or small, impact product delivery. When guided by on-brand Principles, your people can perform consistently to create unrivaled customer experiences that no amount of marketing can match.

HOW PRINCIPLES OPERATIONALIZE AND CLARIFY VALUES

For nearly a century, Toyota has been training its people to see every problem as an opportunity. Employees learn to utilize a series of investigative problem-solving tools that help their teams learn from design flaws and improve products.[11]

One of Toyota's behavioral tools is the Five Whys analysis, which employees use to identify the underlying cause of a problem. When something goes wrong, team members ask why the problem happened. The answer to the question forms the basis of the next "why" until they trace the chain of causality to the source. These actionable steps help employees push past assumptions and surface-level symptoms to find the root cause.

NORMALIZING THE RIGHT BEHAVIOR

Most people aren't wired to ask "why" over and over again. That's a behavior Toyota intentionally instills in its employees. Some of your Principles may also involve counterintuitive behaviors—such as embracing failure, going the extra mile, thinking outside the box, and taking risks. To normalize these behaviors, talk about them regularly with your staff. If you want your team to take risks that lead to more

---

11   "5 Whys: Getting to the Root of a Problem Quickly," *MindTools*, accessed November 1, 2020, https://www.mindtools.com/pages/article/newTMC_5W.htm.

innovation, discuss recent mistakes in your staff meetings. Create space for people to share a risk they took the previous week. Encourage a sense of safety for them to talk about risks that ended in failure. Then discuss what lessons the team can learn.

Go a step further by incentivizing employees to take bold, creative risks that align with the brand. Celebrate the team members who failed after they took a calculated risk to benefit the organization. Turn it into a low-stakes competition by having everyone vote on the best (or worst) on-brand risk, and award the winner with a free coffee or an offbeat prize that rotates to other team members every week. Whatever the reward, it should be a simple gesture to remind your people to take the creative risks your brand needs for successful innovation.

You can also normalize on-brand behaviors by publicly acknowledging employees who demonstrate your core values. When a team member's actions and decisions exemplify the brand, recognize them in an internal newsletter or all-hands meeting.

Create opportunities for peer-to-peer recognition, too. Allow your staff the chance to nominate coworkers who demonstrate your values consistently, and create opportunities to recognize their on-brand contributions.

Model and Clarify Your Principles

[Ted]

I once met the CEO of a Silicon Valley start-up who sat on the board of one of our nonprofit clients. The CEO's company had a value for servant leadership. But his employees were struggling to translate this value into their day-to-day decisions. So the CEO wrote a memo about a time he saw someone in the company living out this value. It happened when several employees went on a business trip and the airline upgraded one of the executives to first class. That leader turned around and gave his premium seat to the lowest ranking person he was traveling with.

This example of servant leadership was so clear—so visceral—that his staff immediately understood the point. They told it over and over again until it was embedded in their minds that servant leadership means being willing to give up something you value and treat others better than how you treat yourself.

That's the level of clarity you need to equip your people to bring the brand to life and deliver it to your customers. Values are only as effective as they are clear. The best brands maximize the impact of their values by translating them into explicit, actionable, on-brand behaviors.

[Mark & Ted]

SHOW, DON'T TELL: HOW TO MAKE A BIG SPLASH WITH YOUR PRINCIPLES

Another way to model your Principles is to choose one and go big on it. Patagonia, a retailer of iconic outdoor gear, prioritizes its employees, their families, and the planet. Since 1983, the company has modeled this value by providing subsidized on-site childcare centers for its employees. Parents pay partial tuition, but Patagonia fronts the bulk of the cost.[12] As a result, nearly 100 percent of new parents come back from maternity or paternity leave, which reduces lost productivity and saves recruitment and training costs. The benefit also boosts employee engagement and work quality.[13]

But this signature perk goes beyond financial savings. It's a loud expression of the company's commitment to people and the environ-

---

12   Bruce Anderson, "5 'Ridiculous' Ways Patagonia Has Built a Culture That Does Well and Does Good," *LinkedIn Talent Blog*, September 27, 2019, https://business.linkedin.com/talent-solutions/blog/talent-connect/2019/5-ways-patagonia-built-ridiculous-culture.

13   Ibid.

ment.[14] By caring for its employees and their children in a big way, Patagonia shows that it's serious about creating a healthier planet for future generations.

[Mark]

At Historic, our "go big" Principle is having fun in what we do. Why? Because I have no boundaries (which is something I'm working on) and I work hard, and most of our employees are the same way. As leaders, Ted and I want to make sure our staff can get away from work and have fun.

One way we do that is by giving our employees an annual $1,000 stipend for vacation. There are limits on how they can spend the money. It has to go toward fun activities such as amusement parks, travel expenses to a vacation destination, or lodging. The point is that when they're on vacation, we want them to get away without feeling like they have to sacrifice fun.

[Mark & Ted]

By going big to model your Principles, you prove to your team that you take your values seriously. It shows that the Principles you ask your people to follow are the same ones guiding your own behaviors and strategic decisions. When employees see you and your leadership team living by the same code, it makes a huge impression, reinforces what your organization stands for, and reminds them how to live it out.

---

14 "Core Values," *Patagonia*, Accessed November 1, 2020, https://www.patagonia.com/core-values.

Promote Your Principles by Holding People Accountable

[Mark]

"Don't be sorry," my mother-in-law often says. "Be different." My wife grew up hearing this all the time. Her mom refused to tolerate bad behavior. Instead of hearing apologies, she wanted to see her kids change how they acted.

Culture is what you allow. Anytime you tolerate unacceptable behavior, it shows your people what they can get away with. If you're seeing off-brand behavior consistently in your organization, it's because you've allowed it to persist. The longer you permit that behavior, the sooner it will drive your culture off the rails.

[Mark & Ted]

Put a stop to egregious actions by holding your employees accountable. Many leaders and managers struggle to do this. It feels easier to ignore behaviors that seem minor and harmless. But in the long run, these add up to weaken your brand and undermine its performance. There's no point in having values if you don't hold your people accountable to them. Author and strategy consultant Ron Carucci puts it this way: "If a company isn't willing to do the very hard work of embedding its values into every fiber of the organization and hold people accountable for living them, they ought not bother writing them down."[15]

USE YOUR PRINCIPLES TO DEAL WITH TOXIC BEHAVIOR

The CEO of one of our clients had interpersonal conflict eating away at her staff's productivity. We estimated that roughly 25 percent of her

---

15   Ron Carucci, "How Corporate Values Get Hijacked and Misused," *Harvard Business Review*, May 29, 2017, https://hbr.org/2017/05/how-corporate-values-get-hijacked-and-misused.

employees' productivity was being lost to unresolved conflict, toxic triangulation, and gossip.

We worked with the executive to build an aligned culture and tie her organization's Principles to clearly defined on-brand behaviors. In one of our workshops, she tapped into the idea of sunlight, a core element of her brand identity, and created a new Principle about dragging conflict into the daylight. The Principle was easy to visualize, hard to forget, and clear enough for staff to understand how to live it out. It also articulated an organization-wide commitment to stop allowing conflict to stay in the shadows, grow toxic, and hijack employees' time and energy.

CALLING OUT BAD BEHAVIOR: "DON'T BE AN ASSHOLE"

When QuikTrip's former CEO Chester Cadieux heard that some of his store managers were treating their employees disrespectfully, he sent out a memo titled "Practicing the Golden Rule." In the 1984 memo, Cadieux wrote:

> [T]here are minimum acceptable standards in the management of our employees. QuikTrip employees expect and deserve intelligent, positive, factual supervision. They do not deserve to work for an asshole. I am more tolerant of poor operation than I am of poor treatment of employees…[W]e cannot tolerate obnoxious, oppressive, abusive, tyrannical despots (assholes).[16]

At the bottom of the memo, he defined each of the words he had used to describe intolerable behavior:

- **Obnoxious**—highly offensive
- **Oppressive**—unreasonably severe; depressing to the spirit

16 Chester Cadieux, *From Lucky to Smart: Leadership Lessons from QuikTrip* (Tulsa, OK: Mullerhaus, 2008), 87.

- **Abusive**—characterized by verbal abuse
- **Tyrant**—a ruler who exercises absolute power oppressively or brutally
- **Despot**—a person exercising power abusively, oppressively, or tyrannically
- **Asshole**—an easily understood American vulgarity for all the above

For Cadieux, having employees who failed to show respect and dignity to others was such an affront to the brand that it warranted the use of profanity.

ACCOUNTABILITY GOES BOTH WAYS

[Mark]

Whenever my young son, Max, comes into the house, the first thing he does is take off his shoes and leave them by the door. And every time, I remind him, "For the love of God, child, there are only two places your shoes go: under the bench near the front door or in your bedroom closet. Only two places." I've said it a thousand times. I keep saying it, hoping that at some point he'll remember and actually put away his shoes without me having to tell him to. But he has yet to do it on his own.

Then one day, I came home exhausted. I'd been up on my feet all day because we were shooting a video. I sat down in the living room and took off my shoes and leaned back. Max saw. And guess what he said to me: "Dad, there are only two places your shoes go—under the bench or in your closet."

Max hadn't yet internalized the behavior for himself. But I tell you what—he certainly held me accountable to the standard I set for him.

[Mark & Ted]

You'll know that your Principles are beginning to make an impact when your people start holding you accountable to them. The important thing is for them to see that you follow the same code and subscribe to the same behaviors you expect of them.

Promoting Your Principles Externally

Your Principles don't just matter to your employees. They also need to be visible on the outside. Consumers look for authentic brands they can trust. Before buying into what you offer, they want to know your mission and purpose, what drives you, how you operate, where you invest money—the why and how behind what you do. Your audience is less interested in simply reading about your Principles. They want to see that your brand lives out the values you say you stand for.

REI's commitment to getting people outside is more than lip service. They're genuinely motivated to awaken in their customers a passion for the outdoors. REI's OptOutside campaign epitomizes that principled commitment. OptOutside began in 2015, when the company shuttered its stores on Black Friday, one of the busiest shopping days of the year, and encouraged customers to make the day about getting out into nature. REI's brand is so aligned around fostering a love for the outdoors that the company is willing to take a financial hit to live it out.

Costco also tolerates losing profits to stay true to its core values. The membership-only warehouse store promises great deals, which it delivers through bulk items such as bargain-priced bales of toilet paper for less than $20. But Costco's longest-standing deal is the hot dog and soda combo. The warehouse has been selling the $1.50 combo since it was first introduced in its food courts in the mid '80s. The price has never gone up. When a Costco executive complained to former CEO Jim Sinegal that they were losing money on the combo, Sinegal made it clear what he thought about hiking up the price. He told the executive, "If you raise the effing hot dog, I will kill you. Figure it out."[17]

Sinegal knew that consumers get more out of the hot dog combo than Costco does. Even though the company barely breaks even on it, customers leave with an indisputable impression of unbeatable value and service.

How They Do It: MONIKER GROUP

Moniker Group is fundamentally about people. As a collective of design, retail, and hospitality companies, the brand exists to empower the dreams and talents of its team members. The Moniker manifesto states that its mission is to "use the company to build people instead of using people to build the company."[18]

CEO Ryan Sisson's leadership style reflects this Principle. He sees it as his goal to release his employees to grow in their gifts and talents and to push them toward their dreams. "I might have you here for six weeks, I might have you here for thirty years," says Sisson. "My job is to make sure you move closer into your calling than you were when you first started with the business."

17   Todd Matthews, "Costco CEO Craig Jelinek on Shareholders, Costco.com, and Hot Dogs," *425 Business* (blog), accessed November 1, 2020, https://425business.com/costco-ceo-craig-jelinek.

18   "Moniker Manifesto," *Moniker Group*, accessed February 13, 2021, https://www.monikergroup.com/manifesto.

Sisson lives out this Principle every day. His primary role is laying the groundwork to build up talented employees and help them succeed in what they do best. He describes himself as a bulldozer, pushing tasks out of the way so his people can focus on creativity and innovation. By managing finance, marketing, communications, and other responsibilities, Sisson sets his staff on a trajectory to focus on producing. "That way the designers can design and the artists can do art and baristas can just do coffee, and they can just do those things really well," he says.

Other core Principles include cultivating community and creating opportunities for connection and collaboration. Moniker's leadership team is constantly reinforcing these Principles through active feedback and positive reinforcement. "We recognize people every month in our meetings and award individuals who best represent the values of our company," says Sisson.[19]

Four Steps to Operationalizing Your Values

STEP 1: WORKSHOP YOUR VALUES

Now's the time to pull out the tools you downloaded earlier. If you haven't done so already, visit culturebuiltmybrand.com/tools to do so. You'll want to work through the exercises below with those documents on hand.

---

19   Ryan Sisson, interview by Ted Vaughn, December 2, 2020.

Every organization needs about five to seven carefully crafted Principles that guide employees' actions, provide accountability, and drive performance. Start by assessing whether your current set of core values represents your brand. If it doesn't, work with your senior leadership team to go back and identify a new set of on-brand values.

Next, work through the following steps to translate your values into behavior-based Principles. Use the tool below to recast them into actionable behaviors. These Principles should be clear and specific enough for your people to know what behaviors they'll be held accountable to.

To recast your values into Principles, work through the questions below for each one of your current values.

1. What does it cost you if your people don't act on this value?

2. What on-brand behaviors are associated with this value? What does it look like for your people to put this value into practice?

3. How do these behaviors support your brand's success?

4. Which of these behaviors can you hold your staff accountable to? How will you hold them accountable?

5. Rewrite the value as a Principle that guides your people to drive your organization forward.

It's okay if these Principles are still in draft form. As you and your team work together to define and shape your culture, you can continue to refine them. For now, write out your behavior-based Principles. You'll refer back to these as you go through the next chapters.

STEP 2: GO BIG TO MODEL IT

Once you've added clarity to your brand values and tied them to actionable behaviors, you've got to model them. The Silicon Valley

CEO did this by offering his staff a clear, on-brand example of servant leadership: it means you give away your first-class seat to a less senior colleague. Patagonia went big and modeled its care for employees' families through subsidized on-site childcare.

Go back to the Principles you drafted and choose one to model in some big, jaw-dropping way. Jot down some initial thoughts as you consider the following questions. Don't get caught up perfecting your ideas. Just brainstorm. You and your team can come back to this later to dream about bringing your "go big" Principle to life.

Use the questions below to brainstorm how your organization can model one of your Principles.

1. How should your employees behave to live out this Principle?

2. What do you want your people to feel or experience through this Principle?

3. How can your organization go big to show employees that it takes this Principle seriously?

4. What employee benefits—tangible or intangible—can you connect to this Principle?

STEP 3: PROMOTE IT

Promoting your Principles is straightforward. Talk about them in all-hands meetings. Include them in internal newsletters. Incorporate discussions about your Principles into your training, hiring, and review practices. Publicly recognize employees who behave in ways that highlight your core values. Consider going visual with something like Netflix's now famous culture deck, a simple slideshow that walks employees through the company's values, why they matter, and how to live them out.[20]

The point is to infuse your Principles into your regular communications and integrate them into your processes so they're visible and accessible to your people. Don't invest heavily into putting them on your website or in your employee handbook. Most employees don't engage with these platforms daily. Instead, prioritize the mediums that your people interact with regularly such as meetings and communications.

Draft a simple plan for how and where you'll begin promoting your Principles internally. Consider these platforms and opportunities as starting points:

- internal newsletters
- all-hands meetings
- shareable culture decks
- training sessions
- new-hire onboarding
- performance reviews

STEP 4: REWARD IT

Incentivize the counterintuitive behaviors that your culture needs to accelerate the brand. Cultivate an environment where it's safe to take on-brand risks. Reward innovation, and talk openly about failures and what your team can learn from them. You can award people for on-brand behaviors with gift cards, public recognition, or random objects. Rewards don't have to be extravagant or costly. They simply

---

20 Netflix Culture: Freedom and Responsibility," *SlideShare*, accessed November 1, 2020, https://www.slideshare.net/reed2001/culture-1798664.

need to reinforce the decisions and actions that shape the culture you're trying to build.

Work through the questions below to draft a plan for rewarding on-brand behaviors:

1. Which counterintuitive behaviors need to be normalized and incentivized to help your people perform on-brand?

2. How can you incentivize your people to demonstrate these behaviors? What sort of recognition, awards, or rotating prizes can you use to celebrate on-brand behavior?

3. What are the next steps you can take to normalize and incentivize these behaviors in your staff?

Integrating Your Principles into Everything You Do

Your values make up the most foundational layer of your culture. When you tie your values to clear behavior-based Principles, you equip and inspire your people to live out the brand in everything they do. This is the first step in cultivating a Marquee Culture that attracts more customers and turns them into raving fans.

With your Principles in place, it's time to integrate them into your Architecture—the systems and structures that support your staff to deliver on your brand promise. Now buckle up for a field trip to Scottsdale, Arizona, for a close-up view of America's architectural identity.

Your Key Takeaways

- When your people are guided by behavior-based Principles, their actions and decisions create unrivaled customer experiences that do more for your brand than any amount of marketing could.

- Turn your values into clear, actionable Principles that empower your employees to live out the brand and guide them to deliver on your promise.

- Choose one value and go big on it. This shows that you and your leadership team take your Principles as seriously as you expect your employees to.

- Operationalize your values by talking about them often and rewarding your people for putting them into practice.

CHAPTER 4

Architecture

The Structures That Support Your People

ARCHITECTURE:

Organizational systems and structures designed to reflect your brand and support your employees to deliver on its promise

What You'll Learn in This Chapter ⟶

- why your systems and structures are wasting your employees' time and preventing them from doing their best work

- how to hire the right employees and showcase them like priceless pieces of art

- why well-meaning projects create drag on your brand and what to do to fix it

- how $20 at Taco Bell empowers employees for elegant decision-making

Located in the desert foothills of Scottsdale, Arizona, Taliesin West feels as if it has always been there—a natural extension of the landscape that surrounds it. Established in 1937 as a winter home and teaching laboratory, Taliesin West is the work of Frank Lloyd Wright, the visionary credited with shaping America's architectural identity.

Wright and his students built the structure with locally sourced materials and drew inspiration from the desert to create a building perfectly suited for and reflective of its environment. They handcrafted Taliesin

West over two decades, constantly improving upon its design and function. With every change, they stayed true to the architect's original intent: to design a structure that fosters an unrestrained internal experience and brings every element in line with the whole.

Taliesin West brings to life Wright's philosophy of organic architecture based on simplicity, freedom of expression, and sincerity. These architectural qualities are also critical to the internal makeup of organizations. The systems and structures comprising your Architecture—your budget, hiring processes, decision-making, and more—all build toward a singular purpose: to help your employees do great work that showcases your brand.

A Philosophy of Organic, On-Brand Architecture

Organic Architecture is about creating more fluid, efficient, and on-brand experiences for your employees. Top organizations align their systems and structures into a seamless ecosystem that operates like an inseparable extension of the brand. Their employees find their work easier to do, and customers experience a product or service that's authentic to the brand promise.

When we start talking with new clients about lining up their Architecture with the brand, they sometimes ask us to help them build the same systems that have worked for some other organization. But what functions for one brand rarely transfers well into different contexts. Each brand operates in a unique environment. Imagine a house built for the desert. It isn't suited for the rainforest. Varied landscapes call for varied structures. Your organization benefits most from a customized Architecture designed to fit and function in its own context.

We've seen leaders go against our advice and try to copy another organization's idea, shoehorn it into their brand environment, and expect it to function well. But it doesn't work. Their culture eventually rejects it

Lack of Trust Breeds Complexity

and spits it out. If leaders do this often enough, their employees grow frustrated and disillusioned with just about any proposed change.

If you like what you see in another organization's Architecture, first study it and try to understand what makes it successful in its unique context. Then consider how to adapt those winning elements into a structure that fits your own context and supports your people as they deliver on your brand promise. This happens most naturally as you foster simplicity, freedom, and sincerity in your systems and structures.

Simplicity

The internal systems that make up your Architecture are naturally complex, but they shouldn't burden your employees. Organic Architecture involves turning complex systems into carefully designed structures that feel simple and support your employees to do their work with ease and clarity.

Picture a house with all the walls removed. You can see electrical conduits, plumbing, gas lines, and—if you're lucky—a central vacuum system. These elements are normally hidden behind plaster and paint, invisible except at the point of delivery such as a faucet or lightbulb. You don't need to see the pipes and wiring to experience the output. The only visible thing is a utility that is elegant and easy to use.

Organizations invest time and money into designing simple, intuitive systems for their customers. They ruthlessly eliminate clutter from the customer experience. But rarely do they do the same internally for their employees. Instead, they build their organizational structures like a growing family's poorly remodeled house. It starts out as a functional structure for a small family. But to fit the needs of an expanding household, they add an extra bedroom, then a new bathroom. Soon they're renovating the kitchen and converting the garage into another bedroom.

As long as the internal systems keep delivering—as long as everything looks like it's still working—then no one cares what's happening under the surface. But the more rooms they add to the house, the more these systems struggle to meet the demands of the household. It's only a matter of time before the strain damages the systems and sets the whole house on fire.

In organizations, this common approach to growth produces bloated, confusing, and time-wasting experiences that exasperate employees and keep them from performing at capacity. Soon enough, their frustration bleeds into their work, reaches customers, and impacts the bottom line.

Organizations may be inherently complex. But they shouldn't be convoluted. Each unnecessary layer of complexity makes it harder for your people to do their work and for your brand to attract more customers.

HOW LACK OF TRUST BREEDS COMPLEXITY

Organizations tend to get complex because they don't address people issues. Instead of holding people accountable, they create systems and structures to limit and micromanage employees' behavior.

[Mark]

I was once hired by an organization to manage several teams. I had a large staff and a big budget. But during my onboarding, I was told that I couldn't book the conference room, the largest meeting space available, unless a senior executive was invited to the meeting. Why? Because someone had once spilled a Coke in the room and hadn't cleaned it up. Instead of dealing with the situation directly and having a conversation with the offender, the leadership team decided they couldn't trust anyone with the conference room again. They created an organization-wide policy to ensure that no one could mess up the space—a rule that wasted senior executives' time by requiring their presence in every large meeting.

[Mark & Ted]

It's easier to constrain people with red tape than deal with their issues directly. But creating rules for policing employees adds internal clutter. It also exposes mistrust. Employees see when their bosses don't trust them to make common-sense decisions. This has an adverse effect on their attitudes and behaviors, which invariably ripples out to the customer experience. In the end, it erodes the culture and undermines the brand.

REMOVE BARRIERS THAT DRAG YOUR PEOPLE DOWN

If your Architecture weighs down your team with layers of red tape and remedial tasks, your mission will fail. Bureaucracy chokes out the creativity and experimentation that fuel innovation. It introduces so many hoops and hurdles that even your most brilliant brand advocates can lose heart and give up. We know it's unrealistic to spare your employees every bit of bureaucracy, but as a leader, you can work diligently to simplify processes to free up your staff's time, mental space, and energy.

Finances are an area that tends to breed burdensome processes for teams, but third-party tools can help streamline these types of tasks. One of the best-in-class products we use at Historic is a corporate charge card that automates expense reports. Every time an employee makes a purchase on their company card, they receive a text with the charge amount and a prompt to send a photo of the receipt, which it uploads to its system. There's no chasing down receipts. Managers don't have to hassle employees to submit their expenses. Everything is automated, from reminders and receipt capture to reporting.

Meanwhile, employees in some organizations spend several hours every month reviewing clunky expense reports generated by outdated or low-cost software. Leaders think they're saving money by choosing the cheapest platform, but the real cost of low-budget, inefficient solutions is the cumulative negative impact it has on your employees. Unnecessary bureaucracy compromises your brand by diverting your employees' time and energy away from the work you need them to do to win over your audience.

The goal isn't oversimplification. Some structures need to be complex to keep people from making serious mistakes. After all, you don't want one of your employees to be responsible for a high-stakes failure such as the false ballistic missile alert that sent the entire state of Hawaii running for shelter.[21]

At the end of the day, your systems and structures should release your team to do incredible work instead of blocking them from producing greater results for your brand. Work with your leaders and managers to limit paperwork for your team, remove remedial tasks, and turn overbearing processes into seamless, on-brand experiences. Change won't happen overnight, but even the smallest improvements you make now will benefit everyone in the long haul.

Freedom of Expression

When your brand is integrated into everything you do, it acts like a guardrail helping your team stay on target. Within the chosen parameters, your employees should be allowed the freedom to innovate and push past roadblocks to accelerate your brand.

---

21   Johana Barr, Adam Nagourney, and David E. Sanger, "Hawaii Panics After Alert About Incoming Missile Is Sent in Error," New York Times, January 13, 2018, https://www.nytimes.com/2018/01/13/us/hawaii-missile.html.

HIRE, CURATE, AND SHOWCASE THE RIGHT PEOPLE

People do great work when they're empowered with freedom, trust, and responsibility. If you hire great people, then you'll have no reservations about giving them the freedom they need to contribute their best to the brand.

Think of hiring as collecting art. World-class art collections are well planned and expertly curated to tell a cohesive story. Each object has individual value and meaning, and it contributes to the larger narrative. When you hire the right people, you can showcase your employees like pieces of art that have worth not only in their own right, but also for the meaning and clarity they add to your brand.

But most organizations are more like cluttered closets than art collections. Leaders focus on hiring candidates with the right résumés instead of looking for people who will contribute to the brand in a big way. On top of that, managers often don't know how to onboard new hires and develop their ability to contribute more meaningful work to the brand. The result can be a team that more resembles a collection of kitschy souvenirs and figurines that don't fit the context of the brand. No matter how talented and qualified your team, if you haven't equipped them to work on-brand, then giving them more freedom won't produce the results you need.

THE RIGHT PIECE OF ART IN THE RIGHT CONTEXT

Freedom of expression only works when you've got the right people in the right place contributing excellent work for the brand.

The culture of Southwest Airlines is built around releasing employees to deliver fun to its customers.[22] That's why the company takes a long

---

22   Kevin Freiberg and Jackie Freiberg, "20 Reasons Why Herb Kelleher Was One of the Most Beloved Leaders of Our Time," *Forbes*, January 4, 2019, https://www.forbes.com/sites/ke vinandjackiefreiberg/2019/01/04/20-reasons-why-herb-kelleher-was-one-of-the-most-beloved-leaders-of-our-time.

approach to hiring, making sure to find fun-loving candidates—such as flight attendants who can rap[23]—while weeding out the rest.

The wrong people still slip through the airline's hiring process. A new hire coming from another airline might have a spotless performance record. On paper, they're well qualified to work for any company in the industry. But if they're not a good fit at Southwest, they don't last long.[24] Their departure often has nothing to do with their skills or performance. It's just that they're the wrong piece of art in the wrong context.

MAKE SPACE FOR THE TROUBLEMAKERS

To drive results, your employees need some degree of freedom to push the culture so that it keeps moving the brand in the right direction. Giving your team freedom creates space for them to work on unconventional projects that have great potential. Google's unofficial 20 percent rule allowed employees to spend a portion of their time working on passion projects they believed could benefit the brand. Some of the company's most profitable breakthroughs, such as Gmail, came out of the 20 percent policy.[25]

Giving your employees freedom doesn't always produce stand-out work. The more freedom you give, the more you can expect your teams to fail. Our simple solution: plan for failure. Develop a project that isn't critical to success but still extends the mission, such as reaching a new audience. Let your employees experiment and push the boundaries of their abilities on that project. If it succeeds, then everyone wins. If

---

23 Neil Baron, "Southwest's Rapping Flight Attendant and the Power of a Value Proposition," *Fast Company*, March 27, 2013, https://www.fastcompany.com/3007485/southwests-rapping-flight-attendant-and-power-value-proposition.

24 Patrick Lencioni, "United Airlines Was Broken Long Before That Doctor Was Dragged Off a Flight. Here's What It Can Do Next," *Inc.*, May 4, 2017, https://www.inc.com/patrick-lencioni/united-airlines-cultural-failure.html.

25 Jillian D'Onfro, "The Truth About Google's Famous '20% Time' Policy," *Business Insider*, April 17, 2015, https://www.businessinsider.com/google-20-percent-time-policy-2015-4.

it fails, the organization will still go on, and your team can evaluate, learn, and move forward. In the end, you'll have fostered a culture of freedom and created a safe place where employees know it's okay to fail when they take well-calculated risks that align with the brand.

Sincerity and Integrity

Your team needs trust and an ongoing sense of safety to create amazing work. And for your team to have trust, you as a leader have to give it. The way you give trust is by being transparent and leading with sincerity, integrity, and heart. Every time we see leaders default to more transparency, it creates long-lasting relationships and results in better work and a more productive team.

Gail McGovern, president and CEO of the American Red Cross, took the helm of the iconic relief and humanitarian aid institution in 2008. At the time, the organization was $600 million in debt. As she and her executives put together a comprehensive plan to revive the 720-chapter organization, McGovern's team created a process that allowed them to listen to and receive feedback from their people—all thirty thousand employees along with hundreds of thousands of volunteers. They created a long buy-in process that helped constituents in chapters across the US feel heard and able to contribute to a final plan to build a better organization.[26]

"If you want to lead," McGovern wrote, "have the courage to do it from the heart."[27] You can't fake heart. Executives who lead from the heart demonstrate an ability to listen and show care in ways that serve the brand. They model trust, humility, and courage—and nurture these traits in their people.

---

26 Gail McGovern, "Lead From the Heart," *Harvard Business Review*, March 2014, https://hbr.org/2014/03/lead-from-the-heart.

27 Ibid.

Systems and Structures

The purpose of your Architecture is to serve the brand and help employees fulfill its promise. In this section, you'll learn about aligning your mission-critical structures—your hiring and firing, benefits package, budgets, decision-making, and leadership structures—to support your team and, in turn, your brand.

PEOPLE OPERATIONS

While Human Resources traditionally focuses on policies, administration, and litigation avoidance, People Operations takes a more holistic approach. It prioritizes cultural health and takes the view that developing employees is critical to supporting the brand. In People Operations, work is designed around keeping employees engaged.

Your organization may not be big enough to have a dedicated People Operations department or even an HR person. As a senior leader, you may be in charge of People Operations by default. But regardless of the size of your organization or its leadership structure, you need someone who ensures that your internal employee experiences such as hiring and benefits line up with your brand.

Hiring and Firing

In traditional hiring, leaders look for people with the best résumés and experience. But this approach rarely builds high-performing teams that produce great on-brand results. The key is to filter your candidates through your Principles to hire employees who can emulate your brand. Otherwise, you waste time and money onboarding the wrong employees.

But even the best on-brand hiring strategy isn't foolproof. Great brands still wind up hiring people who aren't a good fit. Their solution? Offer quitting bonuses.[28] These bonuses incentivize staff to decide how much it's worth sticking with the organization. Discontented employees get a chance to self-select out, sparing the organization unnecessary drag on the brand, while team members with a strong sense of engagement stay on to produce greater work.

Keeping disengaged employees comes at a cost. Companies with low engagement have higher rates of turnover as well as lower productivity, profitability, and customer loyalty.[29] One Gallup study estimated that keeping a disengaged team member costs the organization 34 percent of the employee's annual salary.[30]

[Mark]

In one of my previous roles, I had a high-performing employee who had worked for the organization for years. But he felt disengaged and burned out, and he couldn't see beyond the list of changes he wanted to happen in the organization. I thought I could help by listening to his complaints and making many of the changes he asked for.

After a year of accommodating him, I woke up one day only to realize that the culture had shifted from under my feet and was dragging down the brand. I had altered so much for my employee's sake that our values and structures no longer lined up with the brand I was tasked to build.

28 David Burkus, "Why Amazon Bought Into Zappos's 'Pay to Quit' Policy," *Inc.*, June 15, 2016, https://www.inc.com/david-burkus/why-amazon-bought-into-zappos-pay-to-quit-policy.html.

29 "What Is Employee Engagement and How Do You Improve It?," *Gallup*, accessed February 10, 2021, https://www.gallup.com/workplace/285674/improve-employee-engagement-workplace.aspx.

30 Karlyn Borysenko, "How Much Are Your Disengaged Employees Costing You?," *Forbes*, May 2, 2019, https://www.forbes.com/sites/karlynborysenko/2019/05/02/how-much-are-your-disengaged-employees-costing-you.

[Mark & Ted]

It's not the end of the world if you hire an employee who adversely affects your culture. You may not be able to offer them a lucrative quitting bonus. But you do have to take action, whether that means intentionally helping them find their fit in your brand or firing them.

While onboarding new hires, Jay Desai, CEO of health technology startup PatientPing, clarifies the company's expectations for work, communication, and termination. On day one, he tells new employees that his team hired them in good faith, believing them to be a good match. But when the day comes that their performance, attitudes, or behaviors don't measure up for brand impact, then the company will start working on the employee's exit from the organization.[31]

As you let people go, your brand values should set the tone for termination. At the beginning of the coronavirus pandemic, Airbnb laid off about two thousand employees, nearly 25 percent of its workforce.[32] In a memo to his staff, CEO Brian Chesky reaffirmed the brand's value for its people and committed to doing as much as he could for employees affected by the cuts. His team offered a minimum of fourteen weeks' base pay for each laid-off employee and twelve months of health insurance. The company also built a reverse-recruitment program and reassigned a team to help former employees find new jobs.[33]

Whatever your processes for hiring and firing, they need to attract and retain the people who can produce brilliant outcomes that support the brand.

---

31   "The Indispensable Document for the Modern Manager," *First Round Review*, accessed November 2, 2020, https://firstround.com/review/the-indispensable-document-for-the-modern-manager.

32   Danielle Abril, "Airbnb to Cut Nearly 2,000 Employees Due to the Coronavirus Pandemic," *Fortune*, May 5, 2020, https://fortune.com/2020/05/05/airbnb-cuts-nearly-2000-employees-due-to-coronavirus-pandemic.

33   "A Message From Co-Founder and CEO Brian Chesky," *Airbnb*, May 5, 2020, https://news.airbnb.com/a-message-from-co-founder-and-ceo-brian-chesky.

Benefits Package

Every employee touches your benefits package. That makes it a powerful carrier of your brand. If you lead a small organization such as ours, then you're probably limited in the benefits you can offer. The good news is that you don't need to go over the top. All it takes is a bit of creativity to craft a package that connects your people to your brand.

At Historic, we encoWurage our team to constantly learn new strategies and develop their skills. Our team is small, so our development and training offerings look a little different from what you'd find at a larger agency, but we do provide opportunities for free online training that employees can take at any time.

Another favorite benefit at Historic is Travel Pizza. When a team member goes on an overnight work trip, we send their family pizza the first night so they don't have to worry about dinner.

An executive of a community-driven organization told us how they keep a well-stocked collection of greeting cards for staff members. Employees have unlimited access to the collection, whether they need a last-minute birthday card for a family member or a thank-you note for a coworker. This simple, practical offering helps team members engage and participate in the organization's commitment to building a strong sense of community.

Your benefits package doesn't need to be extravagant, but it should reflect what your brand stands for and point your people to what's important.

BUDGETING

Time after time, we've seen leaders expect wildly different outcomes from doing the same thing over and over again. This happens surprisingly often with budgets. In one nonprofit, we saw senior executives set ambitious performance goals at the start of every year. But they never changed the budget to invest in those goals. Each year they funded the same projects and wondered why they ended up with the same mediocre results and underperforming brand.

An aligned budget puts resources where they need to be to reach brand outcomes. That's why Netflix pays top dollar for the best talent. They compensate employees at the top of the range for their personal market to attract and retain the most exceptional people. No other company pays better than Netflix, so staff consistently perform as if their jobs depend on it.[34]

Budgeting for top talent also feeds into Netflix's culture of freedom and responsibility. The company entrusts its employees to make decisions without the approval of higher-ups. Executives know that this freedom sometimes leads to failure, but it also encourages employees to take exceptional and informed risks that keep the brand ahead of the competition.

Budget Your Time, Not Just Your Finances

Consider the ways you and your team budget your time too. How you spend your time should reflect what you value, whether that's service and community, the environment, or professional development.

During his tenure as CEO of Amazon, founder Jeff Bezos often assigned an employee to shadow him for a year or two. This shadow advisor sat in all of Bezos's meetings to learn as much as possible about every aspect of the company. Most of Bezos's shadows went on to become high-performing senior executives in the company.[35]

---

34 "Netflix Is a Team, Not a Family," June 23, 2020, in *Land of the Giants*, produced by Vox, podcast, Apple Podcasts, https://podcasts.apple.com/us/podcast/netflix-is-a-team-not-a-family/id1465767420?i=1000479218645.

35 Eugene Kim, "Jeff Bezos' 'Shadow' Advisor Position Is Empty for the First Time in Years," *Business Insider*, January 23, 2020, https://www.businessinsider.com/jeff-bezos-shadow-advisor-job-vacant-list-past-shadow-advisors-2020-1.

If your organization claims to value cultivating new leaders, then you need to budget time for leadership development.

DECISION-MAKING

Kodak's epic demise has often been blamed on its inability to keep pace with digital technology, but we see it as a failure of their culture, which blocked the decision-making processes that could have led to greater innovation.

Kodak's culture hadn't always been an obstructive force. The company's origins were rooted in world-class innovation when, in 1888, George Eastman patented the first roll of film, an invention that would make glass plates obsolete. Kodak's culture also cultivated the conditions that allowed one of its engineers to prototype the first digital camera in 1975.[36]

But along the way, executives grew complacent with the company's success. As leaders of one of the most valuable companies in the country, they lost sight of their brand purpose to help people connect with loved ones through "Kodak moments." Instead, executives came to view Kodak first and foremost as a film company—and for good reason. Film cost little to produce, and the company enjoyed a high margin on developing it. With film, executives had a lucrative ecosystem generating big profits. So when Kodak engineers presented their breakthroughs in digital photography, leaders had a tepid response. They didn't want breakthroughs. They wanted film.

The engineers warned that it was only a matter of time before digital photography outpaced film, but it was too late. The culture had already shifted, leading executives to ignore the warnings of their forward-thinking innovators most attentive to the urgent demands of

---

36 James Estrin, "Kodak's First Digital Moment," *New York Times*, August 12, 2015, https://lens.blogs.nytimes.com/2015/08/12/kodaks-first-digital-moment.

the market. Rejecting an opportunity to reinvent the brand to deliver its promise through digital photography, Kodak leaders cut off their engineers from lines of decision-making and opted to stick with film.[37]

If you aren't bringing the right people to the table when decisions need to be made—if you and your leadership team are isolated from the voices of those closest to your customers—then you'll stall your brand and miss out on your people's greatest contributions.

[Mark]

When I worked at Taco Bell as a high schooler, my boss had two mantras he hammered into us. First, he was always talking about how we had a competitive edge because we weren't just another fast-food joint selling hamburgers. Second, he wanted customers to come back. So if we messed up an order, we had up to $20 to fix it. It was that simple. Every employee was empowered to give away twenty bucks worth of food, which is a lot of money at Taco Bell. That policy differentiated us from the competition and gave us the agility to make quick decisions.

[Mark & Ted]

No matter who has the final say in your organization, your structures should have clear, simplified, and accessible lines of communication for employees closest to the point of delivery to speak to decisions. Identify the decision-making processes that exclude your employees' feedback. Then redesign them to give the right employees the freedom and agency they need to inform the right decisions.

---

37 James Estrin, "Kodak's First Digital Moment," *New York Times*, August 12, 2015, https://lens.blogs.nytimes.com/2015/08/12/kodaks-first-digital-moment.

How to Decide When to Kill a Project

Healthy organizations eliminate. If your culture and brand are well integrated, you and your team will know when it's time to end something. It'll also be easier to say no to ideas that don't support the brand.

Organizations lacking clarity around brand often clutter their mission with ineffective projects. Executives in these types of organizations tend to say yes to nearly every well-meaning idea, even if it doesn't support the brand purpose. Without accountability to on-brand performance, they allow highly invested employees to pour their hearts and souls into pet projects that don't align with the mission. Naturally, leaders value the investments of these purpose-driven stakeholders, so they allow their people to do nearly anything they want, thinking it won't hurt anyone.

But it hurts the brand. It creates misalignment and disintegrates the brand promise. Letting staff run free with off-brand projects drains resources, creates drag on culture, and undermines the customer experience.

Saying no begins with brand and culture alignment. Work with your team to clarify your brand and define your purpose. Infuse your Principles into every part of your Architecture so your people know how to do their work. By getting everyone on the same page, it'll be easier to kill projects and ideas that don't align with your brand strategy. When your entire team understands what it takes to fulfill your promise, decision-making is faster, easier, and more efficient.

LEADERSHIP STRUCTURES

The way you lead has the power to single-handedly build up your culture or tear it down. Brand-elevating leadership is about developing and unleashing your people to take the risks that drive innovation.

[Ted]

I was once brought in to redesign the leadership structure of a large luxury brand. The organization had a solid reputation for great design. The senior executive leading the design team was a genius who had worked at the company for years. His designs had raked in millions of dollars for the company, and his reputation in the industry made him critical to the brand. But as a senior leader, he couldn't manage his team, and the whole design department was falling apart.

We worked together to find an organizational leadership structure that reflected their brand purpose and empowered this key player to do even greater work for the brand. We settled on a solution that involved removing his leadership responsibilities while keeping him in a position to pour into the design team as a mentor and senior resident artist. His new role allowed him to excel at what he did best instead of forcing him to be a team leader simply because of his seniority. The design team is now setting higher standards of efficiency, innovation, and productivity for the rest of the organization.

[Mark & Ted]

When you have leaders who create drag on your culture, take a look at your leadership structure. In some cases, you simply need to fire them. Other times, you may have the right person in the wrong position. If the leader brings significant value to your brand, look for ways to redesign your structures to maximize their contributions and to unleash them to produce greater results.

Having the Right Architecture

Attracts the Right People

Hiring the right people, releasing them to take risks, budgeting the things that matter—these aspects of your culture combine to create an

Architecture that empowers your teams to do amazing work and bring in more customers. They also act as a magnet to attract great talent.

The best candidates want to know why you hire, where you put your money, what makes you tick—how and why you do things. They investigate your culture to see whether your internal structures support your team to live out your values, mission, and purpose.

In a world of global health crises, climate change, and financial instability, more and more people are looking at whether an employer stays true to its mission.[38] If you want top talent, then your candidates need to see that you are who you say you are and that your brand reflects it inside and out. Everything you do needs to build up to an attractive culture that fosters an authentic brand and inspires the right employees.

How They Do It: NICO'S BARBER SHOP

As a young entrepreneur running his first business, Rajiv Patel took the traditional approach to hiring. He selected candidates whose résumés and experiences made them look like the most capable candidates. After hiring them, he then tried to change them to fit the culture he was trying to build.

But it didn't work. He couldn't change people. Patel eventually realized that if he hired someone who didn't align with his culture from the start, he'd never be able to get them to fit.

So when Patel founded Nico's Barber Shop in Gilbert, Arizona, he was determined to hire people based on culture. He didn't set out to hire the best barbers because he knew that cutting hair is like all skills: it can be learned and mastered. Instead, Patel filters new-hire candidates based on two traits, neither of which have anything to do with cutting hair. He hires people who are:

- **Humble:** they work hard, show up on time, and, most importantly, are willing to give and serve others while continuing to learn and master their craft.

- **Empathetic:** they care about customers and colleagues, and they're great at customer service.

These core values drive the hiring process at Nico's Barber Shop. By hiring based on these two traits, Patel ends up with employees who buy into the brand's commitment to serve customers and the community. They're more engaged with their work, and they consistently go above and beyond to represent the brand's mission. No employee is in it for themselves. They're quick to show care toward others and eager to give and serve. "That is the most important thing to me—that everyone is 'give first,'" says Patel. "I don't have any takers. Everyone is a giver."[39]

You can teach new hires to be great at cutting hair. But having a clear and consistent culture? That comes from hiring the right people.

---

39 Rajiv Patel, interview by Mark Miller, November 25, 2020.

How to Get Started Aligning Your Architecture

An aligned Architecture is key to building a Marquee Culture that empowers your people to unleash the full potential of your brand. In the last chapter, you refined your values and drafted them into behavior-based Principles. Now we'll help you apply these Principles to the systems and structures that make up your Architecture.

If you're seeking a comprehensive overhaul of your Architecture, we recommend you work with an experienced agency that can provide customized solutions to maximize your brand strategy. Otherwise, using the tools and resources from culturebuiltmybrand.com/tools as a guide, go through the following exercises to identify the practical steps you can take to experience the immediate benefits of brand and culture alignment.

STEP 1: PEOPLE OPERATIONS

Your employees are your most important brand asset. When you've got the right people and they're engaged with your brand, they become top performers who produce amazing outcomes. Work through the questions below, following along on your tool, to identify simple ways to integrate your brand into your hiring, firing, and benefits package.

Focus on just one Principle, or answer the questions for each of your Principles.

→ **Hiring**

1. Describe the ideal employee who exemplifies this Principle. What behaviors, attitudes, and characteristics do they have?

2. What questions and scenarios can you pose in interviews to determine whether a candidate can live this out?

3. Write down the next step you need to take to filter candidates against this Principle.

→ **Firing**

1. When have you terminated employees whose performance or attitude consistently failed to measure up to this Principle?

2. How does your brand inform your approach to letting an employee go? What could it look like to stay true to your brand while firing someone?

3. How can you reinforce this Principle in your communications with your staff after letting someone go?

4. What step will you take to align your termination process with this value?

→ **Benefits Package**

1. How can you infuse this Principle into your current benefits package? Consider updating the language surrounding your benefits or tweaking certain perks so they better reflect what's important to your brand.

2. What new benefits can you offer that showcase this value and engage your staff with your brand? No need to go over the top. Your benefits simply need to reflect the brand.

3. What benefits are your remote team members missing out on? How can you bridge the gap and design benefits to help them experience this Principle?

4. What's the next step you'll take to line up your benefits package with your brand?

STEP 2: BUDGETING

How you spend your money shows what you value as an organization. If you want to push your brand forward, then invest more resources into areas you've targeted for growth. As Hamilton sings in the eponymous Broadway hit, "When you got skin in the game, you stay in the game."[40]

Open up your budget and go through the following questions to align your spending so that it fuels growth where it counts most to your brand. Focus on just one Principle, or go through the questions for each Principle.

1. How is this value reflected in your current budget?

2. What sorts of on-brand initiatives can you fund to integrate this Principle into your budget?

3. Which on-brand initiatives have you neglected to budget sufficiently?

4. List any line items that don't support your brand outcomes. How will you initiate discussions about terminating these items?

5. What projects and initiatives elevate your brand? How will you budget time and resources toward these areas?

6. Write down your next couple of steps for aligning your budget with your brand.

STEP 3: DECISION-MAKING

Decision-making should incorporate feedback from employees closest to the point of delivery. You can start doing this by making sure everyone on your team knows how decisions are made. Open up your decision-making processes to give employees opportunities to contribute mission-critical information. Also coach your leaders to collect feedback from people closest to the action. The goal isn't to generate endless

---

40 Leslie Odom Jr., Lin-Manuel Miranda, Daveed Diggs, Okieriete Onaodowan, and the Original Broadway Cast of Hamilton, "The Room Where It Happens," track 28 on *Hamilton: An American Musical*, Atlantic Records, 2015, mp3.

discussion and make every decision by consensus, but to give employees clear processes for sharing input that builds a better brand.

Take a look at how decisions are made in your organization and go through the following questions. To gain a fuller understanding of how your organization can better align its decision-making, work through some of these questions with key members of your leadership team and staff.

1. Briefly summarize how decisions are usually made and who has the final say on your teams.

2. Is there transparency around your decision-making processes? How do your employees feel about these processes?

3. Are there appropriate levels of open communication in your decision-making processes? Where do you need to increase communication and clarity around decisions?

4. Is your decision-making efficient, or do decisions get dragged out and endlessly discussed to the point of frustration? How can you apply your Principles to inform and streamline on-brand decision-making?

5. What's your process for killing projects and ideas that don't advance the brand? How can you reinforce your Principles to say no to off-brand initiatives?

6. What's the next step you'll take to bring your decision-making in line with your brand?

Now You've Got Permission to Play

We know that Architecture can be the hardest layer to put into place when building a Marquee Culture. But with systems and structures that reflect your brand, you give all the other elements of your culture permission to play.

Next up, get ready for some space-themed inspiration from our favorite fun makers at NASA.

Your Key Takeaways

- Your internal operations—everything from budgets to hiring to decision-making—should reflect your brand with simplicity, freedom of expression, and integrity.

- Your Architecture isn't an end in itself. It's a means to serving the brand and equipping your employees to produce amazing results.

- When you design your systems and structures to reflect your brand, you create a context that equips your people to deliver consistently on its promise.

- Restructure your hiring processes to filter your candidates according to your brand values, and use your Principles to terminate employees who don't drive on-brand results.

- Consider whether your decision-making structures constrain your people, and redesign them to ensure your employees can deliver mission-critical information where it counts.

CHAPTER 5

Rituals

Experiences That Energize Your People

 **RITUALS:**

Repeated, experiential activities that reinforce what's most important in your organization and create a sense of joy and renewed energy around your brand

What You'll Learn in This Chapter ⟶

- how NASA's top rocket scientists reinforce the brand through pumpkins and space robots

- why shared activities have the power to create joy and excitement around your brand

- how Rituals engage employees and equip them to draw more customers and turn them into loyal brand advocates

- how to boost your brand by creating new Rituals and fertilizing your employees' grassroots activities

- how to differentiate Rituals from routines, and what to do when a Ritual starts to lose its magic

Every October, teams of engineers at NASA's Jet Propulsion Laboratory (JPL) in Pasadena, California, take a break from building space robots to carve jack-o'-lanterns that take weirdness and precision to a whole other level. Employees apply their engineering know-how to mock up science-inspired creations with flashing lights, moving components, and space-themed pop culture references.

One year, a team of rocket scientists created an Apollo Lunar Jack-o-Lander. It emitted faux smoke as audio voice-over from the actual Apollo lunar landing played in perfect timing with the pumpkin's careful descent. Another team entered a pumpkin that faked the moon landing in front of a green screen in a mock film studio—a salute to the theory that the landing on the moon never happened. Other engineers transformed their pumpkin into a UFO that beamed up a miniature cow.[41]

The pumpkin carving contest isn't an officially sanctioned activity. Employees use their own resources and do all the design and planning in their off time. On the day of the contest, they clock out for lunch and have one hour to sculpt and engineer their creations.

So why do engineers at JPL, a $2.5 billion federally funded research and development center, pay for supplies out of their own pockets to carve pumpkins during their lunch hour? Because it's a chance to take the same skills they use to put rockets into space and apply them to an unorthodox activity like creating extraterrestrial jack-o'-lanterns. JPL's managers could have labeled the annual pumpkin carving contest as a waste of energy and a nightmare to clean up. Instead, executives allowed it to grow into a culture-building tradition that elevates the brand and reinforces the behaviors that drive NASA's success.

Rituals generate enthusiasm around what is most important about a brand. They energize employees around the values and behaviors that differentiate the brand from the competition and keep it ahead of the pack. Whether they're company-led or employee-driven, such as JPL's pumpkin carving contest, strong Rituals inspire shared joy

---

41   "NASA-JPL Holds Its Annual Pumpkin-Carving Contest," *Jet Propulsion Laboratory*, October 30, 2019, https://www.jpl.nasa.gov/news/news.php?feature=7529.

in the brand and turn employees into invested advocates who work harder and bring in more customers.

The Genius of Rituals

The JPL pumpkin carving contest creates a sense of purpose, camaraderie, and partnership around the brand through a creative and unconventional activity. Everyone enjoys the Ritual—whether they're on a team trying to out-engineer the others or on the sidelines watching the whole thing go down. Participation is optional, but few employees turn down the chance to watch their colleagues apply their rocket-building talent to pumpkin carving.

The contest also creates a sense of ownership for staff. Employees organize and run the activity themselves, and it allows them to celebrate the brand. The contest highlights what JPL teams are all about in their day-to-day work: meticulous attention to detail, resourceful decision-making, innovative problem-solving, and outside-the-box thinking. These are the same brand-defining behaviors that helped NASA engineers find a $5 solution to a problem that nearly cost hundreds of millions of dollars.[42]

HOW RITUALS REINFORCE ON-BRAND INNOVATION

In 2007, NASA discovered a critical flaw in the Constellation Program's Ares 1 rocket.[43] During launch, the crew capsule would vibrate so much that astronauts couldn't read the digital displays. If they couldn't read the displays, they couldn't fly the vehicle.

---

42   Brent Rose, "How NASA Solved a $100 Million Problem for Five Bucks," *Gizmodo*, January 31, 2012, https://gizmodo.com/how-nasa-solved-a-100-million-problem-for-five-bucks-5880850.

43   Keith Cowing, "First Stage Design Problems Arise for NASA's Ares 1 Rocket," *SpaceRef*, November 16, 2007, http://www.spaceref.com/news/viewnews.html?id=1244.

Engineers mocked up several plans to fix the problem. They considered installing springs to dampen the excess shaking. They prototyped motors to fire in a pattern that would counteract the vessel's vibrations. But both of these solutions would take years to develop.

Then one team of engineers came up with a low-cost solution. Instead of redesigning the entire structure, they discovered they could strobe the little display to flash in sync with the vibrations, appearing to freeze the image so astronauts could see it clearly. For a few bucks, they bought a motor to produce the strobe effect—and it worked. The astronauts could see the display perfectly despite the vibrations.

There's a world of difference between carving pumpkins and engineering a solution for a $445 million space-bound crew capsule, but the annual Ritual of turning pumpkins into UFOs gives these rocket scientists a chance to take the behaviors they use for innovating stellar solutions and apply them in a creative, culture-reinforcing activity.

The Competitive Advantage of Rituals

Every leader wants their employees to feel like stakeholders in the brand. But rarely do they create opportunities that give their people a sense of ownership. Rituals are the key to doing that. They generate excitement around the brand and engage employees with a greater sense of investment in the organization. When team members are engaged, they work harder and produce better results in line with the brand. This leads to more consistent delivery on your brand promise, which affects your bottom line and turns your customers into loyal advocates.

Great Rituals also sustain culture and highlight Principles in simple, authentic ways. They give employees a clearer idea of what the brand is about, how to live it out in their daily work, and how to make decisions in the best interest of the brand. Rituals can also build stronger teams and create a deeper sense of community and collaboration. This makes larger organizations feel smaller, warmer, and less corporate.

How Rituals Are Born

Rituals can be initiated either from the top of your organization or from the grassroots, such as the JPL pumpkin carving contest. With a combination of both top-down and employee-led Rituals, you equip your team with fun, tangible ways to live out your Principles.

TOP-DOWN RITUALS

Three times a day, employees at Chez Panisse, a legendary Berkeley restaurant, sit down to enjoy a preservice meal together. The Ritual reinforces a fundamental aspect of Chez Panisse's mission: to create a place for people to gather around the table.[44] Family meals aren't rushed, and they involve all hands on deck. Cooks, service staff, office employees, and team members work together to prepare the meal and clean up. Younger chefs are put in charge of the menu so they get a chance to experiment and hone their skills. The time and money that goes into these family meals add up. But the Ritual pays off in strengthened team relationships, a deeper sense of belonging, and ownership in product delivery.

To energize and inspire your team to produce great results, you need to invest in and create opportunities for employees to engage with the brand. One of the Rituals we have at Historic is our annual Staff Camp, a shared learning experience spread over two or three days. We fly in our remote team members, collaborate on a special in-house project, and invite an industry expert to share with our team. Staff

---

44 Olivia Terenzio, "Day 26: The Importance of Staff Meal in a Restaurant," *OpenTable*, January 26, 2015, https://restaurant.opentable.com/news/features/day-26-importance-of-family-meals.

Music
Club

BREAK-UP JAMS

AFTERNOON JAZZ

HAIR METAL FOREVER

TEENAGE NOSTALGIA

Camp also includes a game night, dinner at a local restaurant, and commemorative swag. This top-down Ritual allows us to extend our mission to our team. It's an opportunity to invest in our employees' learning, strengthen our sense of belonging, and update everyone on where we're headed as a brand.

GRASSROOTS RITUALS

To create your Marquee Culture, you need a mix of both top-down and employee-led Rituals. That means not only creating Rituals that reinforce your brand, but also fertilizing the ones that spring up from the grassroots. If an employee-led activity aligns with your brand and fits the culture you're trying to build, then encourage it and give it space to grow.

A grassroots Ritual we've fertilized in our own company is the Historic Music Club, and it works great for our dispersed team. Every Tuesday during our team huddle, someone shares a favorite album with the rest of the staff. We all listen to it throughout the week, and at our next huddle, we each weigh in and give our reviews (Mark always shares the angsty emo stuff he grew up with. Ted's taking us through his top jazz albums).

The Historic Music Club started with our staff wanting to connect with team members across multiple locations. It didn't come from either of us in leadership. We could have responded by telling our employees that we had work to do and couldn't spend time talking about music albums. Instead, we fertilized it with resources to make it grow. We turned it into a real-time shared team experience by sending Sonos speakers to our remote employees. Now they can tune in and listen to whatever we're playing in our office. By tapping into what our employees initiated, we boosted the Ritual to strengthen community and connection, which makes collaboration across locations easier.

Grassroots Rituals crop up when you and your leadership team allow your people to innovate, try new things, and invest energy into expressing the brand. You have to be willing to let employees have fun and put energy into keeping the activity alive. This spirit of volunteerism transforms staff-led activities into powerful Rituals that can turn your team into a more passionate, engaged workforce.

Types of Rituals

Internal awards, fun competitions, new-hire onboarding—these Rituals energize your people around your brand. They're often unconventional and carry an element of surprise and delight that strengthens their sticking power.

INTERNAL AWARDS

Internal awards celebrate your most valuable internal ambassadors. To function as brand-reinforcing Rituals, internal awards should spotlight brand evangelists—team members who consistently put your Principles into practice and exemplify your brand. Avoid using these to recognize top performers based on measurable indicators of success. There's a place for performance-based awards. But to build a Marquee Culture, your Rituals need to celebrate those who contribute in a big way to what your brand stands for, regardless of how well they're hitting performance indicators.

[Ted]

While I was on staff with a large nonprofit, our team created a Ritual called Principled Heroes. Employees secretly nominated peers who went above and beyond in living out the organization's brand. Then a few times a year, we selected a new Hero from the pool of nominees and celebrated them in a staff meeting.

People never knew when the celebration was going to happen. Employees would gather for our staff meeting, then someone would announce that it was Principled Heroes Day, and everyone would start cheering. The element of surprise motivated people to attend staff meetings so they wouldn't miss out on the chance to celebrate the brand's biggest heroes.

[Mark & Ted]

CULTURE BUILDERS

Culture-building Rituals keep your brand's purpose front and center. They bring employees together, connect them to your mission, and help them engage with what's most important about your brand.

Every month at Historic, we randomly select a team member to send greeting cards to our clients. It helps our employees step away from their day-to-day tasks, put their focus on the people we serve, and engage with our mission to help client brands do more good.

Parties and celebrations are also great culture builders. Since we're big on fun at Historic, we go all out on our annual Christmas party. We treat our team to a fancy meal, and then we do something creative together. In past years, we've done a tasting with a wine producer from France, roasted a batch of coffee at a local roastery, and had a mixologist help us craft our own signature cocktail. One year we went to a printer and learned to do letterpress.

[Mark]

After one of these Christmas parties, an employee said to me, "I wish we could do that every month." I told her we could, as long as everyone was fine with Taco Bell and a Costco sheet cake each month. But then we'd miss the whole point of the Ritual. Our over-the-top Christmas party says something about our brand that a Taco Bell buffet can't: we work hard, we play hard, and we go for really great quality. We're all about creating products and experiences that are as distinct as our brand. This value is so important to us that we do what it takes to prove it to our clients—and our staff. Our culture-building Rituals are all about emphasizing what we stand for.

[Ted]

TEAM-BUILDING COMPETITIONS

At JPL's annual pumpkin carving contest, the competition is fierce, but the point of the contest isn't who wins. The purpose is to energize people around the brand through collaboration, teamwork, and fun. Organizers support these priorities by keeping the stakes low: the only thing winners get is a year's worth of bragging rights.

I once supervised a group of talented creatives and engineers. To help them grow as a team, I planned regular Adventure Trips—group activities that involved creative problem-solving, learning to do something new together, and a friendly dose of competition. I planned the trips off the grid so my staff never knew when they would happen. Once I surprised them with a Top Chef-inspired competition where they got on teams and judged each other's food. Another time we rented sailboats, learned about sailing, and got to race each other. Every Adventure Trip was unpredictable, over the top, and surprising, and each one stretched the team's creative skills and energized their sense of collaboration.

[Mark & Ted]

NEW-HIRE ONBOARDING

New-hire Rituals are a chance to make a powerful first impression and help your employees immediately engage with your brand.

Google affectionately refers to its new employees as Nooglers. Nooglers wear Google-branded beanie hats, which makes it easy for other employees to welcome the new hires into the company. This ritualized peer-to-peer onboarding allows more seasoned team members to take part in the new-employee cultural orientation, and it helps Nooglers experience the brand from day one.

[Mark]

At a previous job, I launched a rite of passage for new hires after they'd been on the team for three months. Once they hit ninety days, I presented the new employee with a Nerf gun as a way to say, "You've made it this far. You've got what it takes. Work hard, play hard, and watch out."

[Mark & Ted]

Rituals for Remote and Dispersed Teams

Remote employees miss out on the natural transmission of culture that happens on co-located teams. To engage your remote staff, use third-party digital tools such as Slack or Google Meet to create virtual touchpoints reinforcing your brand. Here are some ideas to help you extend your brand across dispersed teams:

- Host virtual all-hands meetings every month to celebrate on-brand achievements and learn from calculated risks that either failed or drove innovation.
- Create a chat channel where people can share brand-related content, news, and ideas.
- Mail out new-hire welcome kits.
- Regularly send remote employees your latest swag, a gift card for their birthday, or a book related to your industry.
- Host competitions highlighting the behaviors that make your brand great, such as photo

caption contests to reward creativity or virtual
escape rooms to reinforce problem-solving.

- Have team members take a personality test
  together and share their individual results.

- Encourage employees to meet up for on-the-clock
  virtual lunches or breakfast sessions to talk about
  industry-related challenges and opportunities.

- Create a channel where people can track their ninety-
  day goals and give each other tips and encouragement.

Keeping everyone on a dispersed team engaged is one challenge.
Another is creating a sense of gathering and camaraderie. Offsite
employees miss out on the casual banter and watercooler conversations that help them build rapport with colleagues and strengthen
their sense of investment. But you can simulate the watercooler effect
virtually. Here are ways to connect people on dispersed teams:

- Create chat channels where employees can banter over
  favorite topics such as food, pop culture, and news.

- Host virtual happy hours and include a game you
  play together, or have one person demonstrate
  how to make their favorite cocktail.

- Send everyone on your team a tasting kit, then
  schedule a time to do a virtual tasting together.

- Encourage informal hangouts, such as virtual team
  lunches, pet introductions, and book clubs.

- Host a short virtual huddle every day or once a week with
  a "no work talk" policy to encourage casual conversations.

Rituals versus Routines

The best Rituals aren't meant to fulfill a work-related function or help someone perform a task. They're about renewing a sense of shared purpose and designing creative touchpoints for your team to experience the brand.

Routines, on the other hand, are rote, perfunctory, and automatic. They help employees accomplish a task, but they don't connect people to the brand or reinforce your culture. Routines are useful, but they often feel mundane or even clinical. When your people can run through an activity on autopilot, they're engaging with a routine—not a culture-building Ritual.

We've worked with deeply invested, well-intentioned leaders who mistake routines for Rituals. They try to build a sense of community by dedicating a significant amount of time in their meetings for employees to share personal information unrelated to work. In organizations with an aligned culture built on trust and clarity, this sort of ritualized personal sharing can feel relevant and appropriate. But in misaligned organizations, these activities don't motivate employees. If staff feel obligated to participate, then personal sharing turns into a mandatory routine that needs to be checked off before moving on to the next task.

Mandatory activities aren't necessarily bad. They simply aren't Rituals. Imagine what would happen if JPL suddenly required each of its six thousand employees to carve pumpkins every Halloween. The activity would lose its powerful spirit of volunteerism, turn into a routine, and fail to build a culture that supports the brand. A strong Ritual allows employees to opt in or out. When the shared experience generates joy and excitement, it'll be so compelling that staff won't dare miss it.

What to Do with Tired Rituals

Rituals don't have to last forever. When they stop energizing your team, then they no longer serve their purpose and should be modified or retired.

Here's how to tell the difference between an effective Ritual and a tired one. A strong Ritual generates buzz within your organization. Employees count down the days until it happens. They don't want to miss it. That's how you know you've got a Ritual that's doing what it's supposed to do. But if employees make excuses or take time off on days you've scheduled a Ritual, then kill the activity and start over.

We've seen executives ignore when to retire a Ritual. Even though the activity doesn't delight employees, leaders hold on to it in hopes that it will somehow produce a better outcome. But doing the same things over and over again while expecting different results will not get you the thriving brand you want. You'll end up wearing down your employees by trying to disguise a routine as a Ritual, draining their motivation and sense of excitement.

GOOD RITUAL, BAD RITUAL

One of our clients told us about their annual Christmas party. They had a small budget for the celebration and used most of it to pay for the catered lunch. Unfortunately, the budget wasn't enough to pay for a *good* catered lunch. In private, staff complained about the mediocre meal. Some employees skipped the food line altogether.

But the party wasn't all bad. It involved a fiercely competitive dessert competition, which strengthened the organization's sense of community. Participants brought homemade desserts, and a panel of judges from different departments entertained the rest of the staff with mouthwatering details of each decadent entry. Employees raved about the winning desserts for weeks. Invariably, as the next Christmas party drew near, staff bantered over who could outbake the previous year's winner.

The dessert competition was the obvious highlight. The rest of the poorly executed party felt cheap. Executives would have been better off saving their money, scrapping the catered lunch, and elevating the dessert competition as the focus.

How They Do It: NICO'S BARBER SHOP

"Look good, do good" is more than a slogan at Nico's. It's the basis for Rituals that give employees a chance to live out the brand's commitment to service.

Every quarter, team members take a morning to give haircuts to boys and girls at Child Crisis Arizona, a nonprofit that provides emergency shelter, care, and support for vulnerable children and families. "We want to create a legacy on giving and making our world better," says Nico's owner and founder Rajiv Patel. "Cutting hair is just our way of making it happen."[45]

Patel's barbers look forward to the Ritual as an opportunity to serve. "I've never had anyone say, 'Oh man, we're going to be at the Child Crisis Center for four hours,'" says Patel. "Instead they wake up at 7:00 a.m. and drive down to the center and set up and do it— and they love it."[46]

45   "Meet Rajiv Patel of Nico's Barber Shop in Gilbert and Mesa," *VoyagePhoenix*, May 7, 2020, http://voyagephoenix.com/interview/meet-rajiv-patel-nicos-barber-shop-gilbert-mesa.

46   Rajiv Patel, interview by Mark Miller, November 25, 2020.

Nico's Barber Shop also partners with other nonprofits that package and distribute food to families in developing nations. With every haircut, Nico's donates a meal to feed someone in need. Since opening in 2018, they've donated tens of thousands of meals to people around the world.

"We want people to look good, but we also want to do good," says Patel. "That's what we're about. It encompasses what our mission is. We are constantly looking for new ways to give back."

Four Ways to Create Authentic Rituals

If you don't have Rituals that help your staff experience renewed creativity, joy, enthusiasm, and ownership in your brand, then work through the following steps to start creating some new ones.

STEP 1: ASSESS YOUR TOP-DOWN RITUALS

With your tools from culturebuiltmybrand.com/tools on hand, take a look at your existing company-led Rituals. List any activities you and your leaders have initiated for your staff. Include internal awards, activities that build your culture, competitions, and new-hire Rituals.

Choose one Ritual and answer these questions:

1. Does this activity inspire, surprise, and delight your employees?

2. Which Principles does it elevate and help your people experience?

3. How does it help your staff engage with your brand?

4. How do your employees feel about the Ritual? Do they look forward to it, or do they treat it like a mandatory routine?

5. If it resembles a routine, either terminate the activity or write down ways you can modify it into an engaging Ritual that connects people to your brand.

STEP 2: CULTIVATE EMPLOYEE-LED RITUALS

Now list grassroots activities in your organization. These are often off the grid, so you'll have to dig to find them. Enlist your managers and other staff to help you identify regular employee-led events such as book clubs, lunch-hour activities, informal get-togethers, interdepartmental competitions, and pranks.

Choose one grassroots Ritual and answer these questions:

1. Does it reflect your brand?

2. Which Principle(s) does it support?

3. How can you nurture this activity into a culture-building Ritual?

A word of caution: Don't hijack these activities by taking them out of your employees' hands. When cultivating grassroots Rituals, the best approach is often the lightest one. Sometimes all it takes to transform an employee-led activity into a powerful Ritual is a bit of public recognition. You may want to start by simply affirming the activity in front of your entire staff and pointing out how it reflects your brand.

STEP 3: CONSIDER REMOTE TEAM MEMBERS

For your remote employees, you'll need to be a bit more creative with your Rituals. Use digital communication platforms to extend the reach of your Rituals and create a sense of belonging for your remote team members. Here are some ideas to get you started:

- Create a chat channel for sharing brand-related news and content.

- Host competitions that reinforce on-brand behaviors.

- Encourage virtual meet-ups to share industry-related tips and best practices.

- Mail your swag and brand-related content to your employees.

- Have a regularly scheduled session to celebrate your team successes and learn from failures.

Brainstorm your own ideas for Rituals that extend your brand to your remote staff.

STEP 4: CREATE NEW RITUALS

If you're like most leaders, you may need to build Rituals from scratch. This is a chance for you and your team to have fun and experiment as you come up with activities to engage your staff.

Choose one of your Principles and then brainstorm potential Rituals that can help cement it in the minds of your employees. Think about friendly competitions, team-building activities, onboarding Rituals for new hires, and internal rewards.

1. List activities that can engage employees around this core value.

2. Which of these hold the greatest potential to delight your staff and foster new energy and excitement around your brand?

3. How do these ideas point back to the Principle?

Your next step is to run your top ideas past a few employees to feel out whether it will fly as a brand-boosting Ritual. Then, come up with a plan for piloting the Ritual. Be sure to include how you'll get buy-in from your team leaders and how you'll terminate the Ritual if it doesn't engage your people.

Now take a moment to draft a simple plan for testing your new Ritual.

One Final Rule for Creating Your Rituals

When it comes to Rituals, we have one last rule: have fun. Keep the stakes low, and permit your people to opt out. When you hit on the right Ritual, it'll be an experience so energizing that your employees can't help but join in on the fun.

In the next chapter, discover how one underperforming employee was simply living out the brand when he fell asleep on the job.

Your Key Takeaways

- Rituals create joy and excitement around your brand and give your employees a renewed sense of energy to drive brand success.

- Ritualize your internal awards to celebrate brand ambassadors—and create team-building activities, friendly competitions, and seasonal celebrations that reinforce what your brand stands for.

- Fertilize your employee-driven, grassroots Rituals to give your people a sense of ownership in the organization.

- Identify the Rituals that have gone stale or are burdening your team. Either kill the activities or modify them to energize your staff.

- Use digital platforms to extend the reach of your Rituals to your remote employees and create a sense of community on dispersed teams.

CHAPTER 6

Lore

The Sticky Stories That Shape Us

LORE:

The canon of stories that circulate within your organization and reflect the most positive, negative, and even mundane ways your people experience your culture

What You'll Learn in This Chapter ⟶

- how Lore showcases your culture at its best—and its worst

- why some stories stick and how they enter the canon of your organizational Lore

- who makes your Lore, and how to get them to create the right Lore that drives results

- why negative, off-brand stories proliferate—and what to do to fix it

- how stories about $40,000 failures and secret speakeasies accelerate your brand

[Mark]

I had just started a new job at a large nonprofit. As I met my coworkers, one person was introduced as the guy who got caught taking a nap on a couch in an empty office. I thought it was strange that the first thing I was told about another employee was something negative. But in the weeks that followed, I heard that story get repeated over and over again. Leaders brought it up in staff meetings. People in other departments told it to me. Instead of disciplining the employee, the entire staff responded by regularly subjecting him to public shame. Everyone thought it was funny, and it made them feel better about themselves—because no matter how bad their own performance was, at least they didn't fall asleep on the job. Their organization-wide response allowed the guy's failure to set a low bar for performance.

But it didn't line up with how executives talked about the brand. According to leaders, the workplace was a high-performing environment that demanded employee loyalty. "If you don't see it as a privilege to work here, then there's a line of people waiting to take your place," they often told us. Their words signaled that you had to work your tail off to stay employed. If you didn't, they'd fire you.

Meanwhile, the organizational Lore told a completely different story: if you underperform and fall asleep on the clock, you won't lose your job. You'll face public humiliation, but, barring that, you can keep doing whatever you want. So much for the line of high achievers waiting to take our jobs.

[Mark & Ted]

Lore is made up of the stories your people tell over and over again. These stories shine a spotlight on your culture, revealing how your team members truly experience it. This is where misalignment becomes clear and obvious. The stories that make up your Lore highlight whether your culture is boosting your brand or disintegrating it.

Every Organization Has Lore

Stick around in an organization long enough, and you'll start to hear its Lore. The anecdotes shared in the office kitchen or in private chat channels—these are the stories that evolve into Lore and become part of the organization's oral history.

Stories are barometers of brand and culture alignment. They reveal which values are most active in your culture—regardless of whether those values are on-brand or off, good or bad, inspiring or disruptive. Lore exposes your organization's true culture. The stories circulating among your employees point to what's working and what needs to change. What matters is whether those stories are elevating your brand or tearing it down.

How Stories Turn into Lore

In many organizations, executives hold a certain view of their culture that doesn't align with how their people experience it. Employees' stories expose this misalignment. Instead of reflecting the executives' perceived culture, the Lore reveals how staff experience the culture in their daily work.

As a leader, you can tell great stories that cast your brand in its best light, but you can't force them to enter your organization's Lore. Your employees determine the stories that stick. They repeat the anecdotes that most resonate with their experiences, cementing them into the canon of your Lore.

One senior executive told us about an unofficial mantra at his organization: "You're just a plane ride away from losing your job." Whenever the CEO traveled, he was on the lookout for talent. Everyone knew this to be true because several employees had actually been hired after the executive had sat next to them on a plane, deemed them more qualified than a current team member, and offered them a job before the plane landed. The story became Lore not only because it was true, but also because it accurately reflected the organization's internally competitive culture.

Your Employees Determine the Stories that Stick

Types of Lore

Lore has the power to cement fundamental truths in the minds of your employees. It can remind people of what your brand stands for, or it can point back to your origin story. Lore is often operational, instructing your employees on how to carry out their work or avoid making mistakes. It can also rally your team around a specific future vision for the brand.

BRAND-ELEVATING LORE

While moving into his new office, a young Pixar animator found a small door in the wall next to his desk. Behind the door, he found a hidden passageway. The animator did exactly what you'd expect of an employee working for the company that produced imaginative adventures such as *Toy Story* and *Inside Out*. He got on his hands and knees and crawled through the passageway. At the end of it, he found a small room that housed the building's central air conditioning valves. With the help of a few colleagues, he turned the secret nook into a speakeasy and decked it out with lava lamps, animal-print upholstery, and bar supplies.[47]

This simple, authentic story fast-tracked its way into Pixar's Lore. It resonated with employees by clearly showcasing the spirit of exploration and discovery that defines the brand and permeates nearly every Pixar storyline. The Lore was so powerful that it drew celebrities and dignitaries such as Steve Jobs, Buzz Aldrin, and Sasha and Malia Obama to the secret nook so they could experience the brand firsthand.

ORIGIN STORIES AS LORE

Patagonia founder Yvon Chouinard never dreamed of selling outdoor gear and clothing. He just wanted to rock climb. But as a young climber

---

47   Edward Moyer, "Getting In on the Secret of Pixar's 'Hidden' Speakeasy," *Cnet*, May 19, 2012, https://www.cnet.com/news/getting-in-on-the-secret-of-pixars-hidden-speakeasy.

in the 1960s, Chouinard found that the gear didn't measure up to his standards. At the time, the only available pitons, which climbers use to drive into cracks in the face of rock walls, were single-use tools that got left behind stuck in the rock. But Chouinard followed a "leave no trace" philosophy. He wanted a piton that he could remove and use over and over again.[48]

So he bought a used forge, learned how to blacksmith, and started making simple removable pitons. It turned out he was good at it, and he launched a company that would eventually spawn off to create Patagonia, one of the largest outfitters of climbing gear in the US.

[Mark]

I visited Patagonia in Ventura, California, some years back. While I was there, I learned that the company had built its headquarters around the original corrugated tin shed that Chouinard had leased when he first started making pitons. As part of the new-hire onboarding process, new employees got to work alongside Chouinard in the tin shed and learn how to forge their own piton.

Combining its origin story with Ritual, Patagonia reinforces the Principles that have guided the company since Chouinard forged his first piton: a dedication to crafting reusable, high-quality tools made to endure and a commitment to leaving no trace.

[Mark & Ted]

CORPORATE WISDOM AND OPERATIONAL LORE

On-brand stories aren't always positive. Every organization has negative stories in its Lore. The important thing is that those negative

---

48 Yvon Chouinard, "Patagonia in the Making: My Founder's Story," *Branding Strategy Insider*, July 18, 2018, https://www.brandingstrategyinsider.com/brand-patagonia-a-founders-story-and-strategy.

stories impart valuable lessons about how employees can support the brand through their work.

The CEO of a large publicly traded Fortune 100 company told us about botching up some paperwork when he was a young manager. The mistake resulted in an error that cost the company $1.2 million. Once he realized what he'd done, he went to the executive who supervised him, told him what had happened, and said, "I guess I'm fired then, right?"

"Why would I fire you?" the executive responded. "I just invested over a million bucks in training you." Then he charged the young employee to go to each of his peers and show them how to avoid making the same mistake. Doing so ended up saving the company $6 million in clerical errors that year.

Many other leaders would have fired that young employee for his million-dollar mistake. Instead, his boss had the foresight to transform a costly failure into a profitable gain by turning the story into a corporate learning experience.

[Mark]

In one of my first jobs, I was put in charge of marketing and communications for a large nonprofit. I contracted a third party to develop an app for the organization. But I hadn't done my due diligence, and the contractor failed to deliver the app. That mistake left my department $40,000 in the hole with nothing to show in return.

I'm not proud of that story. But I tell it all the time because I want our team to know it's safe to make mistakes (but hopefully not amounting to tens of thousands of dollars). So when our employee hits send on an email and it goes to the wrong audience, she's got perspective: it can't be as bad as my $40,000 failure. Our team knows that it's okay to mess up—as long as they course correct, learn from their failures, and keep the project moving forward.

[Mark & Ted]

Sticky stories such as these are less about reinforcing your culture and more about the operational side: fill out your paperwork, back up your data, double-check your math, and run quality control before you hit send. This type of Lore has the power to turn mistakes into lucrative learning opportunities. Instead of writing off your employees' errors as total losses, transform them into instructive Lore that supports your brand. This helps your team learn from failures and fosters a culture that breeds innovation.

PROPHETIC LORE

Most stories look back at past events. But prophetic Lore points people forward to what you're trying to build. With future-oriented narratives, you can cast a vision of a tangible reality that has yet to be realized.

At Historic, our future vision is based on the belief that brands have the power to influence our society for good. We've worked with hundreds of nonprofits—organizations that, unlike businesses, don't have a transactional service or product to sell to customers. Instead, they offer purpose. We've helped accelerate these brands by infusing that sense of purpose into everything they do and reinforcing the promise they offer to impact communities and contribute to the greater good.

We want to bring these same brand-building methods to for-profit organizations so that their bottom line isn't just about how much money they make, but also about how they treat their staff and their customers. Because then, what would happen in the world? We believe it would become a better place. That's what we're working toward: a future in which every brand we work with—regardless of the type or size of the organization—is so aligned with its mission and purpose that it becomes more profitable and changes the world for the better.

Prophetic Lore inspires. It turns your employees from the current reality toward the future they're helping build—a reality in which your brand is making a real difference for your customers, your community, and the world.

That said, use prophetic Lore sparingly. It needs to be authentic, honest, and directly connected to your brand outcomes. Otherwise, your employees will write it off as an empty promise. If you don't do your part to live out the vision you've cast through prophetic Lore, you'll wind up damaging your brand.

How Lore Drives Brand Success

In his book *What You Do Is Who You Are*, venture capitalist Ben Horowitz shares how an executive at Netscape Communications crafted a piece of Lore that changed how teams made decisions and unleashed innovation. In the early days of the internet, decision-making at Netscape was slow and painful. The process was open to endless debate, and very little work got done. Horowitz describes the all-hands meeting where Jim Barksdale, the new CEO, gave his staff three rules to guide their work:

4. "If you see a snake, don't call committees, don't call your buddies, don't form a team, don't get a meeting together, just kill the snake."

5. "The second rule is don't go back and play with dead snakes. Too many people waste too much time on decisions that have already been made."

6. "And the third rule of snakes is: all opportunities start out looking like snakes."[49]

---

49 Ben Horowitz, *What You Do Is Who You Are: How to Create Your Business Culture* (New York: Harper Collins, 2019), 105–106.

The parable was clear, funny, and easy to retell. It immediately became Lore, and as employees retold the story over and over again, it changed the culture. People started to care less about how decisions were made. Instead, they focused their time and energy on bringing the internet to life through breakthrough technologies like JavaScript and cookies.

The Creative Dimension of Lore

Stories have the power to generate new opportunities for your brand. Take the American Express Centurion Black Card as an example. The Black Card is an exclusive, invite-only charge card for the ultra-rich. With a signup fee of $7,500, and an annual fee of $5,000, it has no spending limit.[50] The card comes with elite benefits including a personal concierge service for when you need to book travel, make reservations at a restaurant, or get sand from the Dead Sea for your child's school project.[51]

But the Lore came before the product. Before the Black Card even existed, rich consumers were circulating rumors that American Express had an exclusive product for its most elite spenders. The idea intoxicated people who had buckets of money to spend. Owning a Black Card turned into the ultimate proof of making it in the world of the rich. American Express saw an opportunity to turn rumors into reality, and the company launched the Black Card as a signature product.[52] That decision has brought in millions of dollars and spun off an entire luxury credit card industry.

---

50   Megan DeMatteo, "Black Cards Are the Ultimate Status Symbol—But What Are They?" *CNBC*, October 15, 2020, https://www.cnbc.com/select/what-is-a-black-card.

51   Yoni Blumberg, "American Express Offers an Elite Credit Card for the Super Rich—Thanks Perhaps to Jerry Seinfeld," *CNBC*, September 11, 2018, https://www.cnbc.com/2018/09/11/the-american-express-black-card-may-exist-thanks-to-jerry-seinfeld.html.

52   "Ultimate Prestige: Getting the American Express Black Card," *Fora Financial* (blog), February 10, 2020, https://www.forafinancial.com/blog/small-business/ultimate-prestige-getting-the-american-express-black-card.

Legends such as these prove just how little control you and your leadership team have over the stories people tell. But when you hear a story that hits the mark, capitalize on it to reinforce the brand promise.

The Gravitational Pull of Negative Stories

The off-brand Lore that circulates in organizations is often toxic. Human nature tends to be drawn to negative accounts about micromanaging supervisors, blame-shifting coworkers, and heartless executives. Toxic Lore proliferates in climates where employees feel like they aren't trusted and are excluded from decision-making. This often happens in organizations with hierarchical models of leadership. Feeling powerless to make decisions relevant to their work, team members seek the cathartic release of frustration by venting to their peers. This background chatter fuels the toxic stories that get told when leaders aren't in the room.

Focusing on the negative is human nature. You can't block your employees from circulating destructive stories. But you can counteract the gravitational pull of toxic Lore by reinforcing on-brand stories that remind your people of the culture you're trying to build.

Counteracting Toxic Lore with Brand-Positive Lore

To counteract off-brand stories, begin by intentionally creating brand-positive Lore elevating the values and behaviors that make your brand great. Curate stories showcasing the culture you're trying to build. Then share them over and over again. Bring them up in meetings. Write about them in your internal communications. Highlight how these stories reflect what you want your brand to be and do. Share them broadly and frequently. For stories to stick, try sharing them between ten and twenty times, or at least every twenty-one days for a year. That frequency will produce stories that none of your employees will forget.

By telling carefully curated stories, you can give your people a crystal-clear vision of how they can help advance your brand.

The Stories No One Wants You to Hear

When you discover stories that don't reflect the culture you're trying to build, take a systematic approach to root them out. Start by listening to your employees' experiences. Then ask questions to understand your culture through their eyes. Finally, cultivate honest, transparent conversations about the state of your culture.

LISTEN TO YOUR PEOPLE

If you don't spend time with your employees, then you're not able to listen to them. This is something every leader struggles with—including us. We get so buried with work that we forget to prioritize listening to our employees, validating their experiences, and responding with the right actions. Don't get so busy that you can't make time to hear your people's stories.

Former Defense Secretary and retired four-star general James Mattis, a.k.a. Mad Dog Mattis, was known for abandoning his comfortable officer's quarters to visit his troops in the trenches and eat with them in the mess hall. Mattis wanted to hear firsthand what was working on the front line and what wasn't. The best way to get that information was directly from his troops.[53]

---

53 Paul Szoldra, "Defense Secretary Mattis' First Message to the Troops Tells You Everything You Need to Know About His Leadership Style," *Business Insider*, January 23, 2017, https:// www.businessinsider.com/defense-secretary-mattis-first-message-to-troops-2017-1.

[Mark]

In our work with various organizations, I'm surprised at how few leaders are willing to simply listen to their people to understand what's going on in their organization. At one organization, I directed marketing and sales. Not once did the CEO invite me to coffee or lunch.

That CEO isn't alone in this area. Most leaders simply don't spend time with their people. At best, they depend on what their department heads and managers tell them, like a game of telephone that muffles ground-level information as it filters up through the ranks.

If you don't take time to cultivate trust and listen to your people, you won't hear the stories that make it into your Lore. Use your one-on-ones to ask questions and solicit feedback from your employees. Ask them to share a story about when they saw the organization hitting the mark on your culture—or when it utterly failed. If other employees share the same accounts, there's a good chance that these are the sticky stories that have entered into the canon of your Lore.

[Mark & Ted]

ASK QUESTIONS TO UNDERSTAND

Next, brush up on your active listening skills and ask questions that investigate the source of a story. Your goal is to solicit as much information as you can: where the story came from, what it says about your employees' experiences in the organization, and how it made it into your Lore.

Before you start asking questions, be sure to foster a safe space for employees to share honestly without fear of reprisal. You can help create a safe environment by making it your habit to regularly check in with your employees. The more often they hear you asking about their experiences, the more likely they'll believe you care.

Be aware that, as a leader, you may be contributing to a culture that is producing toxic Lore. Most employees won't feel comfortable giving their higher-ups honest negative feedback. Try approaching your employees with humility. Be willing to hear hard things. Then own up, and make changes. In the end, you'll help cultivate a climate of trust, care, and transparency with your staff. You'll also help strengthen their sense of investment while discovering how they truly experience your internal culture.

BRING STORIES INTO THE LIGHT

Once you've started listening to your people and have an accurate read on the types of stories being told in your organization, address the ones that are working against your brand. Start by sharing what you've learned with your executives and managers. Bring toxic and unhelpful stories into the light and point out how they don't represent the culture your organization needs to build a successful brand. Then share your vision for the culture you're trying to create—a culture that helps your people live out your brand and do amazing work.

Rooting Out Toxic Culture

To root out the toxic culture that produces off-brand Lore, you still need to go deeper. You can tell the right stories and take the time to listen to your people. But to sustain change, you need a total shift in your culture to align it with your brand.

Your Lore reveals the state of your internal culture. Stories working against your brand often highlight areas where your culture lacks clarity. Other times they expose a leadership style that isn't serving the brand. Sometimes they surface around dysfunctional structures or employees who are adversely affecting your culture.

To counteract toxic stories, you need to rein in your culture and put a stop to off-brand behavior. That can mean firing people, dismantling hierarchies, or making decision-making more transparent, just as we've addressed in previous chapters. As you continue building your Marquee Culture layer by layer, you'll create an environment that inspires your people to perform on-brand and puts an end to toxic Lore.

How They Do It: CLARK

In the early 2000s, a minder from NASA showed up at a Clark work site with a prototyped high-definition (HD) video camera specified for use on the Space Shuttle. It was one of four such NASA cameras in existence.

Clark's client wanted to stream large-scale video projection across multiple locations. But to get image quality big enough for a thirty-seven-foot-wide screen, they needed a video camera with high pixel density. At that time, 4K resolution didn't exist, so the Clark team was looking for an HD camera with as many pixels as possible. They were nearly impossible to find.

But NASA had them. The space agency had contracted Panasonic to invent a camera to monitor space shuttle launches and other components of the space program. Panasonic prototyped four cameras for NASA. Three of them were put on space shuttles. The fourth was a spare. And Clark cofounder and chief engineer George

Clark happened to know someone at Panasonic who knew a guy at NASA who helped them borrow it.

The camera arrived, and Clark engineers set it up to broadcast by a fiber-optic link to a prototyped screen in another location. It worked perfectly. Clark eventually bought the camera from NASA and installed it into the client's production system, thereby inventing streaming image magnification that has become the industry standard for multisite livestream audiovisual projection.

In part, this is a story about innovation and pushing the limits of how things have always been done to figure out how to go further. "Innovation is part of our culture," says Clark CEO Todd Austin. "Where we have always excelled in innovation is figuring out the 'if' and making it work."[54]

But it's also a story about the importance of relationships, a core value and driving force behind Clark's success. Everything they do at Clark focuses on prioritizing people and relationships. So when it came to getting their hands on a NASA-specified camera, they could tap into the relational strength of the brand and turn to whom they knew. Their entire brand is built on relationships. "That's just who we are," says Austin. "That is our culture."

---

54 Todd Austin, interview by Mark Miller, February 12, 2021.

How to Curate Brand-Positive Lore

You can't dictate which stories exist in your organization. But you can decide how you'll respond to them. When off-brand stories surface, take the time to listen to your staff to mine for stories, understand their experiences, and counteract the Lore.

STEP 1: MINE FOR STORIES

Try to spend time listening to your people daily. Don't let busyness rob you of this critical leadership function. Work through the following excercises to find ways to build time into your days for listening to your staff and hearing their stories.

List three specific, measurable things you can do to make more time to listen to your employees.

1. Which one of these will you try first?

2. What steps will you take to act on it?

3. When will you put this into action?

STEP 2: ASK QUESTIONS TO UNDERSTAND

As you listen, ask questions that plumb the depths of the stories you hear. Try to identify the source of the Lore and understand how and why it resonates with your employees. For your staff to feel safe to share, you'll need to ask questions frequently. Use your one-on-one meetings to probe for stories and dig deeper. Avoid taking a confrontational or aggressive approach. Try to gather information objectively to gain a deeper understanding of your culture and its Lore.

To learn about specific stories in your Lore, use these starter questions with your employees:

1. When was a time that you felt the team was really living out one of our brand Principles? When did you see us missing the mark?

2. If someone wanted to know what it's really like to work here, what story would you tell them?

    - What do you think this story says about our organizational culture?

    - What patterns does it reflect in our organization?

    - If you could change something about this story, what would it be?

STEP 3: BRING THEM INTO THE LIGHT

It takes courage and humility to drag toxic Lore into the light. But exposing off-brand stories helps you and your team acknowledge the state of your culture and commit to doing something about it. You may want to work through the following steps with your executives and managers first before bringing unhealthy stories to your entire staff. Here are questions to consider as you prepare to discuss off-brand Lore with your team:

1. How can you share toxic Lore in a way that retains the respect and dignity of those involved?

2. What are some of the key insights you've learned as you asked questions for deeper understanding? How will you share these with your team?

3. What are the weak links in your culture that are producing toxic stories?

4. How will you cast a vision for an aligned
   culture that supports your people and
   produces more brand-positive Lore?

STEP 4: CLARIFY YOUR CULTURE TO COUNTERACT BRAND-NEGATIVE STORIES

After listening for, investigating, and exposing off-brand Lore, counteract it by sharing brand-positive stories and reinforcing the culture you're trying to build.

Fertilize an On-Brand Story

Think about the stories you've heard as you've listened to your employees, and choose one that reflects the culture you're trying to build.

1. Briefly describe the story

2. What Principle does it showcase? How?

3. What platforms can you use to share this story?
   Specify when and where you'll start sharing it.

Share the story broadly and frequently, about ten to twenty times or every twenty-one days for a year.

Reinforce On-Brand Behavior

To counteract brand-negative stories, you also need to reinforce the right behaviors. This happens as you build your Marquee Culture and integrate your brand into every layer. For now, focus on an off-brand story, and identify one Principle you need to reinforce to make this type of toxic Lore a thing of the past.

Think about an off-brand story you've encountered in your organization.

1. Which Principle needs to be activated
   to counteract this story?

2.	How can you reinforce this Principle to help your people live it out? Review the end of chapter 3 for practical ways to model, promote, and reward the Principle.

3.	What next step will you take to better integrate this Principle into your employees' daily experiences?

How Your Lore Can Make the World a Better Place

Lore always points back to your greatest brand ambassadors: your people. Their experiences in your organization affect how they view your brand and how hard they'll work to drive it forward. A Marquee Culture ensures that you end up with stories reflecting your brand at its best and inspiring your employees to help make it even better.

On to chapter 7, where you'll discover how one small word nearly brought down our brand.

Your Key Takeaways

- Stories act as barometers of your culture. They reveal your employees' experiences and point out critical issues that need to be addressed to align your culture with your brand.

- You can't control the stories that become your Lore. But you can decide how you'll take action to turn them into powerful reinforcers of your brand.

- Tap into employee failures by turning them into sticky stories that extend corporate wisdom throughout your organization.

- To understand where your off-brand stories are coming from, take time to listen to your people and ask questions that get to the source.

- Address toxic Lore by identifying the root problems they expose. Then counteract it with positive stories while integrating your brand into every layer of your culture.

VOCABULARY

CHAPTER 7

Vocabulary

Words Create Worlds

VOCABULARY:

A lexicon of clearly defined words and phrases helping your
employees understand what's important in your brand and how
to drive it forward

What You'll Learn in
This Chapter ⟶

- how to translate your intuitive understanding of your
  brand into a powerful lexicon that produces results

- how a customized Vocabulary unique to your brand
  shapes your culture and inspires your people

- why the CEO of the world's biggest hedge fund
  company obsesses about pain

- how organizations perpetuate white noise—and the
  steps to take to fix it

- how to build a Vocabulary that creates bigger
  opportunities for your team to bring your brand to life

[Ted]

Hustle. We love the hustle. As the founders of Historic, Mark and I
decided to put hustle at the core of what we do. But rarely have we
seen one word create such powerful momentum for some employees
while driving others to discouragement and frustration. What was
intuitive to us as leaders wasn't clear to our staff. And for some of

them, living out their own version of the hustle was leading to burnout and toxic behavior.

Hustle isn't about working to the point of exhaustion. At Historic, hustle means when we work, we work hard. We put stuff out. We meet problems and challenges head on. We get more done with less. We learn to work harder and smarter with limited time and resources, constantly looking for ways to be more efficient and innovative.

But as our agency grew, our innate understanding of hustle didn't reach all our employees. Some of our staff thought it meant working more instead of working smarter. They pulled all-nighters to complete projects they should have finished during work hours. Instead of learning to hustle by using time management and productivity tools, they wore themselves down. Soon their frustration started impacting their work, the team, and our brand.

So Mark and I went back to our Principles and reworked them to make it crystal clear that we never stop looking for ways to improve. In meetings, we clarified our unique definition of "hustle." We also started timeboxing, a technique that assigns time limits to specific tasks to help our team focus on real-time problem-solving. This encourages them to view their time as a limited resource so they can learn how to get more done with less.

We never abandoned the hustle. We simply clarified and defined it within the context of our culture to help our staff understand what matters most to our brand.

[Mark & Ted]

Why Your Brand Needs a Vocabulary

Founders, CEOs, and senior executives often have an intuitive understanding of the beliefs and behaviors that should be guiding their brand.

As long as their organization remains small, leaders can usually get by without having to clearly articulate these core beliefs to their employees.

But as an organization grows, it becomes more difficult for that deep awareness of the brand to cascade out and reach every person on every team in every location. In the absence of a basic, customized Vocabulary keeping employees oriented to the brand, leaders unintentionally perpetuate white noise. Lacking the vision and direction of carefully chosen words that drive success, employees work independently of each other—and even against the brand.

Organizations also generate white noise by having too many words in their lexicon. If everything matters, then nothing matters. A Vocabulary that's too large makes it harder for employees to figure out what to prioritize to serve the brand.

Every organization needs a consistently used Vocabulary that builds a common understanding of the key concepts driving your brand. A curated list of sticky words and phrases shapes the culture and reminds employees of what's most important about the brand.

Words as Waypoints

On an average day, more than 1,500 flights fly across the Atlantic Ocean.[55] To manage the busy airspace, controllers assign planes to specific lanes of traffic, much like highways in the sky. Pilots navigate their aircraft to their assigned sky route with the help of beacons and virtual waypoints. These invisible waypoints are like geographical coordinates on a virtual map of the sky, directing planes safely toward their destination.

---

55   "Celebrating 100 Years of Transatlantic Flights," *Eurocontrol*, June 17, 2019, https://www.eurocontrol.int/news/celebrating-100-years-transatlantic-flights.

Words are like waypoints on your map to brand success. They provide a clear trajectory for your day-to-day operations and guide your employees to stay on the right track.

SUNSHINING FAILURES AND FARMING FOR DISSENT

In chapter 1, we shared the story of Qwikster, Netflix's misguided attempt to differentiate its DVD-by-mail service from streaming, a move that led hundreds of thousands of customers to cancel their subscriptions. CEO Reed Hastings eventually admitted that he should never have launched his flawed idea. After Qwikster, he and his executives developed the Netflix Innovation Cycle, a Vocabulary-rich process of vetting ideas to prevent future decision-making disasters.

The Innovation Cycle begins with "farming for dissent" or "socializing" an idea.[56] In this step, Netflix employees solicit feedback from their peers and supervisors, inviting them to openly challenge their proposal. Next, an idea gets tested. After it passes a test run, employees hedge their bets on the idea and launch it. If it succeeds, everyone celebrates it. But if it crashes and burns, the project gets "sunshined." It's brought into the light in a sort of failure forum where the owner of the idea takes responsibility for the unsuccessful project. It turns into a corporate learning exercise as employees systematically discuss where the idea came from, what the process was, and how they'd do things differently next time.[57]

Farming for dissent, socializing an idea, and sunshining failures—these phrases reinforce the company's culture of innovation, transparency, and collaboration. Using these words and phrases helps normalize failure. The Vocabulary reminds Netflix employees that failure is an acceptable byproduct of taking risks to keep the brand ahead of the pack.

---

56 Reed Hastings and Erin Meyer, *No Rules Rules: Netflix and the Culture of Reinvention* (New York: Penguin Press, 2020), 140.

57 Ibid., 157.

MOVE FAST AND BREAK THINGS

For years, developers at Facebook held to its internal mantra, "Move Fast and Break Things." Keeping pace was more important than delaying a product launch to do quality control. The phrase reflected a culture that tolerated untested, buggy products in the name of speed.

In 2014, CEO Mark Zuckerberg announced that his company was adopting the new mantra, "Move Fast with Stable Infra."[58] It signaled a pivotal change for employees: Facebook was no longer exclusively focused on speed. Now it was also committed to thoroughly testing new tools and products before pushing them live.

When you find words and phrases that are producing off-brand behavior and negative outcomes, commit with your team to retire them. Or you can modify them so they guide your people to better perform on-brand.

THINK OUTSIDE OF THE TO-DO

[Mark]

Back in the day when I worked at Taco Bell, it used the slogan "Think Outside the Bun." Everyone on our team (except for Ted) loves Taco Bell, so we adapted the phrase to "think outside the to-do." Every day at Historic, each of us has a list of to-dos to accomplish. That makes it easy to get so focused on individual tasks that we lose sight of the big picture. "Think outside the to-do" reminds our staff to consider everything, not just what's directly in front of them. It tells them to look at their work in the context of the whole project. It challenges them to keep asking big questions to create great work for our clients.

[Mark & Ted]

If you don't have Vocabulary giving your team concrete direction for how to behave and do their work, you're missing out on a powerful builder of

---

58   Samantha Murphy, "Facebook Changes Its 'Move Fast and Break Things' Motto," *Mashable*, April 30, 2014, https://mashable.com/2014/04/30/facebooks-new-mantra-move-fast-with-stability.

culture. Look for the gaps in your brand—the places where your people are consistently failing to meet expectations and serve the mission. If your employees are struggling with focus and direction or simply running up against the same roadblocks, then it's time to refresh your lexicon.

But first, let's broaden our understanding of how Vocabulary builds your brand and how it drives innovation.

How Vocabulary Defines Who You Are

Your Vocabulary is specific to your culture. It points back to your brand and spotlights the distinct ways you operate—such as whether you function like an Olympic sports team, a family, or a room full of competitors. Your Vocabulary also defines the fundamental ways your people carry out their work to deliver on your promise.

Vocabulary isn't the same as jargon. Your Vocabulary is unique to your brand. It describes who you are, how your people behave, and how you stand out from the rest.

THE KEEPER TEST

One of Netflix's most unconventional practices is called the Keeper Test. Managers use the test to evaluate whether their employees are the right people for the job by asking, "Which of my people, if they told me they were leaving for a similar job at another company, would I fight hard to keep?"[59] The test encourages managers to do everything possible to retain top performers. It also helps them identify when they should fire average employees and search for more stellar candidates.

As Vocabulary, the Keeper Test reiterates a shared understanding that Netflix's high-performance culture isn't a family; it operates like an

---

59   Reed Hastings and Erin Meyer, *No Rules Rules: Netflix and the Culture of Reinvention* (New York: Penguin Press, 2020), 186.

all-star professional sports team.[60] Pro teams don't tolerate adequate performers. Keeping mediocre talent drains resources and drags down the team's overall performance. Armed with that understanding, Netflix managers would rather leave a position open so they can find the best person to fill it.

The Power of Words to Create and Drive Innovation

"Words create worlds," Rabbi Abraham Heschel often said. As a young scholar, Heschel barely escaped the Nazi invasion of Poland in 1939. He saw firsthand how the Holocaust didn't begin with tanks and guns. It began with language and propaganda.[61]

Words shape reality, and they move people to act. History proves that they can be used to justify unspeakable human rights violations, but they can also inspire people to live up to something greater. In organizations, words can shine a spotlight on possibilities and opportunities that otherwise might have remained hidden.

PAIN + REFLECTION = PROGRESS

Most people try to avoid pain, but Bridgewater founder and CEO Ray Dalio not only embraces it, but also maximizes it. Pain acceptance is fundamental to the culture of Bridgewater, which is one of the most successful investment management firms in the country. To Dalio and his team, it's impossible to avoid pain, especially if you're pursuing ambitious goals and aiming for higher targets.

A guiding mantra at Bridgewater is "pain plus reflection equals progress," a counterintuitive phrase that forces employees to accept pain as a natural

60 "Netflix Culture," *Netflix*, accessed November 4, 2020, https://jobs.netflix.com/culture.

61 Abraham Joshua Heschel, *Moral Grandeur and Spiritual Audacity: Essays* (New York: Farrar, Straus and Giroux, 1996), viii–ix.

step in the pursuit of success.[62] It shapes the culture by reminding people to push past fear to maximize their potential for the brand.

The company operationalizes Dalio's pain equation through large gatherings where employees air their failures, admit when they're wrong, challenge each other, and share what they've learned from their mistakes. This combination of Vocabulary and Ritual helps employees overcome the fear of pain-inducing failure. It also fosters a culture of radical transparency and risk-taking that drives the brand's success.

HOW VOCABULARY CREATES NEW POSSIBILITIES

People see the world according to the images and ideas created by their words. When you add a word to your employees' lexicon, it expands their view of what's possible, just as Dalio's pain equation opens his employees to harness the positive outcomes of pain. Broadening your team's Vocabulary introduces new opportunities, guides your people to embrace counterintuitive behaviors, and helps them step into bigger challenges to serve the brand.

MONIKER
GROUP

How They Do It: MONIKER GROUP

Moniker Group CEO Ryan Sisson tells about a long-time employee whose performance was falling behind. After several conversations about his work, the staff member was still unwilling to work on becoming a better team player. Just when his manager was about to "transition"

---

62   Ray Dalio, *Principles: Life and Work* (New York: Simon & Schuster, 2017).

him out of the company, the employee chose to leave the design, retail, and hospitality brand of his own accord.

Moniker's use of the word "transition" captures the brand's focus on people, relationships, and community. Transition implies a natural, healthy departure of a team member whose goals, values, and vision no longer align to serve the brand. Similarly, when a Southwest Airlines employee leaves, they're "promoted to passenger." This type of Vocabulary emphasizes value for people and creates opportunities for former employees to stay connected with the brand.

In addition to its informal lexicon with words like "transition," Moniker has an exceptionally rich, intentionally curated Vocabulary surrounding its mission to bring dreams to life. Team members call Moniker the "dream factory," a place where people are empowered to make their dreams a reality. Every year at their annual Christmas party, senior staff distribute "Dreamie" awards to employees who live by the Moniker manifesto, a Vocabulary-rich declaration to "dream a better world and then to build it."[63] Even the Moniker name, which literally means "name," serves as a sort of placeholder for "insert your dream here."[64] It reminds dreamers and creatives that their role in the company is to pursue their passions, push the boundaries of their creativity, and do their best work to make the world a better place.

---

63 "Moniker Manifesto," *Moniker Group*, accessed February 13, 2021, https://www.
    monikergroup.com/manifesto.

64 Ryan Sisson, interview by Ted Vaughn, December 2, 2020.

Four Steps to Curating

Your Customized Vocabulary

A curated Vocabulary should include clear, simple, and straightforward words and phrases that point your people to your brand's purpose and how you want them to operate. Your Vocabulary can include what you call your employees, such as Disney's cast members, Starbucks' partners, or Taco Bell's champions. You can incorporate key words that describe a unique attribute of your culture, such as Historic's "hustle." Your lexicon can also contain carefully crafted, operational phrases such as "farming for dissent" or "move fast with stable infra."

Your organization may already have words and phrases worth adopting into your Vocabulary. As you work through the following tool, review your values and Principles, examine your Architecture, and revisit your Rituals and Lore to search for words and phrases that are already operational within your organization.

Focus on words and phrases that can close your brand gaps—the places where your current culture doesn't align with the vision you have for your brand. As you brainstorm, think about the Principles and specific behaviors that need to be operationalized by your people to get your brand where you want it to go.

Use the tool provided on culturebuiltmybrand.com/tools to work through the exercises below.

STEP 1: IDENTIFY YOUR CURRENT VOCABULARY

1. List some of the distinct words and phrases used frequently in your organization.

2. Which of these differentiate and support your brand and your desired culture?

3. Write down the words and phrases that don't support the culture you're trying to build.

   a. Identify words that aren't gaining traction, perhaps because they're hard to understand or have different meanings for different people.

   b. Look for Vocabulary that produces undesirable behavior and outcomes that drag your brand down.

   c. How will you commit with your team to retire or modify these words and phrases?

STEP 2: GLEAN VOCABULARY FROM YOUR CULTURE

1. Revisit the other layers of your culture (Principles, Architecture, Rituals, and Lore). What words and phrases are embedded in these layers that can be adopted into your Vocabulary? Consider how you operate internally, what you promise customers, your unique Rituals, and your brand-defining values and traits.

2. Which of these words or phrases best describe who you are as a brand?

STEP 3: CRAFT PRINCIPLE-BASED VOCABULARY

Choose one of your Principles and work through the following steps.

1. What words and phrases inform people how to live out this Principle in their day-to-day work?

2. Brainstorm additional Vocabulary that can help employees remember and internalize this value.

STEP 4: PUT IT INTO PRACTICE

1. Out of the words or phrases you've listed, select a few that are most authentic and distinct to your brand.

2. Now you'll need to get feedback from several employees. With whom will you share these words and phrases? How will you ask them for input?

3. When and where will you begin rolling out your curated lexicon once you and your leadership team have settled on the right words and phrases? Write down the specific meetings and communication platforms you'll use to share your Vocabulary.

Shaping Your Desired Culture

Through a Customized Vocabulary

By curating an on-brand Vocabulary, you articulate what your brand is all about and impart it to the people most critical to its success. Once your team has a lexicon supporting your brand, it's important to use it often and consistently so that your employees remember it and allow it to shape their work.

We've spent the last five chapters working on your Marquee Culture layer by layer. We started with the deepest, most foundational layers: the Principles driving your brand and the Architecture supporting it. From there we talked about experimenting with Rituals, fertilizing on-brand Lore, and customizing a Vocabulary that guides your people to work toward brand success. We're about to hit the layer closest to the surface: Artifacts, which are the spaces and objects your people can see and touch. This is where all the layers come together to create the most visible, tangible expression of your culture that allows your people to more fully engage with your brand. Ready to smooth out that final layer?

Your Key Takeaways

- Vocabulary isn't jargon. It's a unique set of curated words and phrases clarifying how you operate and inspiring your people to produce better results.

- New words and phrases can help employees discover greater possibilities to deliver on your promise in a huge way.

- Having too few or too many words in your Vocabulary creates internal white noise. Pinpoint a few defining words and phrases, and then use them consistently to orient your people to your brand.

- Dig into the other layers of your culture to find words and phrases that can help close the gaps between your brand's current reality and where you want it to go.

ARTIFACTS

CHAPTER 8

Artifacts

The Look and Feel of Culture

ARTIFACTS:

The tangible objects at the surface level of your culture helping your people engage and feel a greater sense of ownership in the brand

What You'll Learn in This Chapter ———→

- why swag and logos often fail to boost your brand, and how to design objects that do

- how to bring design thinking into creating Artifacts that move your people

- why no one wants a $10 gift card to the company store

- how to design simple, engaging Artifacts without breaking your budget

Stanford University's Hasso Plattner Institute of Design, also called the d.school, acquired its original bright red IKEA Klippan sofa in 2006, just before their first class of students arrived. Cheap, functional, comfortable, and virtually indestructible, the couch had flair. Its vibrant color epitomized the energy of the d.school's unconventional learning environment. Everything about the couch seemed to embody the creativity that differentiates the school from other departments at Stanford.

As the d.school grew, they purchased more red Klippan couches for their classrooms. They attached wheels to make the couches mobile and keep their spaces flexible.[65] Rumor has it that teams of students and staff sometimes competed in red couch races.

Featured on T-shirts and posters across campus, the red couch has icon status at the d.school. It has evolved into a powerful Artifact symbolizing design thinking and strengthening students' connection with the d.school's brand.

From red couches and office layouts to swag and employee awards made out of thrift store purchases, Artifacts are intentionally chosen and designed to make a statement about who you are. These physical objects express your brand in ways your team can see and touch. They are often visceral and tend to be what employees remember most.

The Most Visible Layer of Your Culture

Artifacts occupy the level of culture nearest to the surface. As the topmost layer of your culture, they reiterate your brand for the people who matter most to your organization's success. Well-designed Artifacts echo your brand and sustain your culture by tangibly pointing out what you value and how you operate. A red couch conveys bold creativity, energy, and functional design—just as one company's indoor football field speaks to a commitment to teamwork.

Right in the center of Keap's headquarters is a bright green artificial turf football field. Executives at Keap, a B2B company providing CRM and marketing automation services to small businesses, aren't extraordinarily fanatical about football, but they do value working as a team and celebrating victories. The football field reminds employees of one

---

65   "Red Couch: Our Longest Living Prototype," Stanford University d.school, accessed November 5, 2020. https://dschool.stanford.edu/redcouch.

of the core values driving the brand: we win together.[66] Employees operate as a unified team, with each player doing their part to help the brand win. That bright green turf is a visual and physical asset shaping the culture by rallying people together.

Types of Artifacts

Artifacts can be utilitarian. Sometimes they're cheeky, and other times sentimental. The important things are they add value and help people interact with your brand. Most Artifacts fall into one of several categories: spatial, operational, inclusive, and high-engagement.

SPATIAL ARTIFACTS

Like Keap's football field, spatial Artifacts bring brand values to life in a big way. They're often prominent and make a loud statement.

[Ted]

I worked with a brand that had several decommissioned red phone booths from London set up throughout the building. The office had just been redesigned into an open-concept floor plan. Most employees who previously had private offices were now working in a shared environment. But staff still needed occasional personal space, and even worse, cell-phone service was horrible outside the building. Executives recognized the need and brought in the red phone booths so employees could take private calls or have a moment of quiet. The phone booths didn't offer a ton of privacy given the sides were made with glass panes. They were also narrow, so you couldn't get too comfortable for too long. Still, the phone booths reflected care for employees, met a real need, and reinforced a culture of transparency.

---

66   "Our Shared Purpose Fuels Entrepreneurial Growth," About, *Keap*, accessed February 15, 2021, https://keap.com/about/culture.

I also worked with a nonprofit running a big fundraising campaign to finance a new building. Just before construction began, they held an on-site celebration with their staff and donors. Everyone was given a permanent marker and a brick to sign their name and write a message. Those bricks were eventually placed inside the new building in high-traffic areas where they could visibly remind people of the sacrifice and investment that had gone into making the building a reality.

[Mark & Ted]

OPERATIONAL ARTIFACTS

IBM's Enterprise Design Thinking field guide is a pocket-size booklet equipping field consultants to apply the company's approach to design. Staff use the field guide to help teams solve problems, innovate, and prototype solutions. It drives employees to focus on brand outcomes while creating and improving products.[67]

Operational Artifacts such as IBM's field guide are usually designed to help employees do better work for the brand. Some organizations do this through annual journals. These branded journals often include a list of the organization's big goals, driving Principles, and key milestones for the year ahead. Such journals may also have sections where employees can write down their own goals, challenges, and contributions to the brand. An intentionally designed annual journal helps employees focus on the big picture and reflect on brand-advancing outcomes throughout the year.

For many of our clients, we've created customized decks of cards that highlight unique details about the brand. One client is all about building strong relationships and fostering a sense of community, so we designed a deck of conversation cards to inspire employees to ask engaging questions and cultivate relational curiosity. Another client

---

67 "Enterprise Design Thinking Field Guide," *IBM*, accessed November 5, 2020, https://www.ibm.com/cloud/architecture/content/field-guide/design-thinking-field-guide.

A high sense of belonging

= a 56% increase in performance.

invests significant resources into unleashing the untapped potential of their people. For them, we created a deck full of questions to help managers discover hidden talents in their employees.

Creating operational Artifacts for your brand doesn't require a big budget. One of our low-cost Artifacts at Historic is a Polaroid wall full of photos of our clients. Every time a client visits our office, we take their photo and put it on our wall as a tangible reminder of our mission to serve the people behind the brands we support.

INCLUSIVE ARTIFACTS

Fostering a sense of belonging yields a big return. Employees who feel valued and included are usually committed to the organization and have more consistent performance. According to research from professional coaching firm Betterup, a high sense of belonging is linked to a 56 percent increase in job performance, a 50 percent decrease in turnover risk, and a 75 percent drop in sick days.[68]

You can cultivate a sense of belonging by creating Artifacts celebrating employees' milestones in your organization. Disney employees, or "cast members," receive special pins celebrating their years of service. Cast members covet these pins and wear them with pride.

Welcome kits also help create a sense of inclusion. They initiate new hires into the culture and help them quickly bond with the brand. A new-hire kit can include a branded mug or water bottle, custom-designed swag, Artifacts unique to their new team, and welcome gifts such as locally roasted coffee and gift cards. Each Artifact in a new-hire welcome kit should say something about your brand. If continual learning is a high value, throw in a book that several other

---

68 Evan W. Carr, Gabriella Rosen Kellerman, Andrew Reece, and Alexi Robichaux, "The Value of Belonging at Work," *Harvard Business Review*, December 16, 2019, https://hbr.org/2019/12/the-value-of-belonging-at-work.

team members have read. If community is your thing, include hand-written notes of encouragement from their new colleagues.

Whenever we hire a new remote employee, we have our staff record and send them welcome videos. In these personalized videos, team members introduce themselves, describe their role, and offer their unique insights into:

- their favorite part about working at Historic
- the biggest adjustment to coming on staff
- the challenges they think we need to work on at Historic
- the areas they can support the new hire
- what excites them about Historic's mission and vision for the future

These personalized videos have made a big difference in our onboarding process and have helped new employees feel an immediate sense of inclusion on the team.

HIGH-ENGAGEMENT ARTIFACTS

High-engagement Artifacts rarely fulfill a practical job function, and employee interaction is usually optional. The purpose of these types of Artifacts is to offer your team members an opportunity to engage with an important part of your brand in a concrete way.

In chapter 4, we shared how one community-driven organization offers employees unlimited access to a well-stocked collection of greeting cards. This Artifact reflects their Principle to care for others and allows their team to engage with that value tangibly. It may not help the organization sell more product, but it does help employees feel more engaged and connected, which means they'll do greater work and draw more customers.

[Mark]

My local REI store has a bulletin board covered with photos curated from employees' outdoor adventures. It shows normal people scaling mountains and doing all sorts of outdoor activities. Located in a high-traffic area where it's most visible to employees, the board reminds the REI team what the brand is all about: helping people live out their passions by getting outside and being in nature.

[Mark & Ted]

Artifacts don't need to be complex. One of the most coveted objects we've seen is a stray bowling pin purchased from a thrift store, spray-painted in a brand color, and awarded at random to different employees throughout the organization. Your Artifacts can be simple and low cost as long as they move your people toward your brand and remind them of what sets it apart from the rest. The point is to engage your team and make your brand contagious.

What Your Swag Says about Your Brand

Anyone can make swag. Select a pen, keychain, or mug—something that doesn't cost too much. Then get a designer to slap a logo on it and call it good. Most organizations approach swag this way. Sometimes this produces an object people love. It may even articulate something about your brand. But most of the time, swag falls flat.

Logo-based swag can help with brand awareness and remind employees of whom they work for. But it rarely differentiates your brand or moves it forward. Why? Because a logo doesn't convey the meaning that leaders often think it does. No matter how clever or obvious its design, it can't carry your brand. Relying on a logo to shoulder your brand identity is asking it to do more than what it's intended to do, and it results in swag that can feel hollow and gimmicky.

Our one rule for creating Artifacts is this: design your swag. Don't just slap your logo on stuff. Create swag so that it says something meaningful about your brand and reinforces your values. Unless it's intentionally connected to your brand, your swag is little more than wasted money.

SWAG THAT MOVES YOUR BRAND

Think about the swag floating around your organization. Does it express your brand in a concrete way? Do your staff even want it? Executives often expect their employees to like whatever they're given. But rarely do leaders think to ask their staff what they truly want. To serve as an Artifact that strengthens your brand, your swag needs to resonate with and appeal to your staff.

We're not saying you can't have swag. Just make sure it's intentionally designed to boost your brand. What you give your people should do more than simply inform them of who they work for. It should excite your people around the brand and remind them what your organization is about.

The Importance of Custom-Designed Artifacts

[Mark]

An organization I worked for gave employees a $10 gift card to the company store on the anniversary of their hire date. But everything in the store was leftover swag, such as $40 branded hoodies and stuffed animals bearing the company logo. No one wanted any of that stuff, even with the $10 discount. It would have been better for the organization to have done nothing at all. Had leaders cared what employees actually wanted, they would have tried to come up with an Artifact truly celebrating their employees' tenure and moving them toward the brand.

[Mark & Ted]

Unlike the other layers of culture, Artifacts require a bit of skill to execute. It takes good design sense to know what people want, what they'll interact with, and what moves them. Doing that well also takes time and effort. That's why we ask each of our clients to make sure their Artifacts are custom designed. We encourage them to work with professionals who can show empathy through design and create meaningful objects that engage staff and articulate the brand.

Our employees love Staff Camp. We get to invest in their professional development, and they enjoy learning together and collaborating on a project. On top of that, they get a little bag of custom-designed swag that includes an exclusive patch for that particular Staff Camp. Our team members receive these patches like badges of honor.

Find some creative people to help design and execute Artifacts reflecting your brand. If you don't have an in-house designer, hire an outside contractor trained in the design thinking approach who can think through empathetic, user-centric solutions.

How They Do It: CLARK

"We don't recommend any solution, especially if it's mission critical, unless we have put our hands on it and tested it out ourselves," says Todd Austin, CEO of Clark, a firm specializing in audio, visual, and lighting (AVL) systems and production design.[69]

---

69   Todd Austin, interview by Mark Miller, February 12, 2021.

That's why Clark invested money and space into creating an on-site testing theater, a spatial Artifact dedicated to inspecting and sampling gear before shipping it to be installed at a client site.

AVL manufacturers ship every piece of equipment with detailed specs. Most of Clark's competitors take these specs and go straight to installation, trusting that the manufacturer got the numbers right. "But we want to test it to make sure it does what they say it's going to do before we put it in a client's room," says Austin.

Clark's engineers spend a significant amount of time in the testing theater. One time, Austin found six hundred feet of cable stretched from the theater to the other side of the building. It was the work of Clark's chief technology architect. He was testing the latency in the cable for that length, making sure the manufacturer's specs were accurate.

When it comes to other Artifacts like swag, Clark employees can't get enough of trucker hats. The branded hats come in four or five different styles. They're fashionable—and utilitarian. Many Clark employees are installation engineers who spend their days sweating in the shop or working at a client site. Trucker hats not only outfit them for the job, but also help them broadcast the Clark brand to the world.

"I had a twenty-three-year-old employee ask for more hats and stickers," says Austin. "And he actually wore the hat and used the stickers. So there you go. It worked. That's brand."

How to Design Artifacts That Drive Your Brand

There's a reason Artifacts comprise the final, top layer of your Marquee Culture. After integrating your brand into the other layers, you'll have a comprehensive, aligned understanding of your brand and a clearer sense of what sorts of objects can engage your people. Otherwise, you risk chasing after gimmicks and settling on Artifacts that do little to inspire your team.

To begin designing your Artifacts, start with your brand gaps. Do a quick survey to identify areas of misalignment where your people still aren't performing on-brand. Then prioritize the gap you want to address first.

Complete the exercises below, following along on your tool from culturebuiltmybrand.com/tools.

STEP 1: IDENTIFY YOUR BRAND GAPS

1. Where is your performance falling short? How are your people failing to move your brand forward?

2. Which of these gaps will you address first for the biggest return?

3. What behaviors do you need to see in your employees for them to start living out the brand?

STEP 2: START SMALL AND SIMPLE

Next, you'll brainstorm ideas. Work through the following exercise to identify existing objects and spaces. Then come up with new Artifacts that can help your employees perform on-brand. Don't overcomplicate this step. Keep it simple, affordable, and manageable.

Brainstorm with Your Team

1.   Gather with your team and send them out to walk
     through your office looking for objects, physical concepts,
     and spaces supporting your brand. When everyone
     comes back, ask people to share what they saw and
     how these spaces and objects articulate your brand.

2.   Brainstorm ideas for new spaces that can be designed
     to serve employees as they advance your brand.

3.   Brainstorm new ideas for tangible objects that can
     help your people interact with your brand. Think
     about operational Artifacts supporting your staff as
     they do their work, inclusive Artifacts fostering a
     sense of belonging, and high-engagement Artifacts
     helping employees interact with your brand.

STEP 3: DESIGN YOUR ARTIFACT

Out of the ideas above, choose one tangible Artifact you believe will
guide your people to live out the brand more fully. Be sure the Artifact
fits your budget. Now you're ready to start designing.

To design your Artifact, work with a professional trained in design
thinking, an approach that produces empathetic, user-centric solutions
by asking questions such as:

- How is someone going to use and interact with this Artifact?
- Does it evoke the desired response, emotion, or feeling?
- Does it align with the brand Principles?
- Does it move the brand in the direction we want to go?

Inspiration and Ideas for Custom-Designed Artifacts

Operational Artifacts

- decks of cards clarifying your culture and supporting your brand
- field notes with operational tips critical to daily work
- annual journals that include the organization's mission and big goals
- cheeky awards passed around to employees who exemplify the brand

Inclusive Artifacts

- pins or objects awarded to employees at key milestones in their tenure
- badges acknowledging achievements within the organization
- new-hire welcome kits with curated items and swag pointing to the brand
- team-specific Artifacts such as fun nameplates or Nerf guns

High-Engagement Artifacts

- community boards showcasing how employees live out the brand

- greeting card collections (bonus tip: use custom-designed cards!)

- beautifully designed coffee-table books highlighting unique aspects of your brand

- a community bookshelf allowing staff to share brand-related resources

Spatial Artifacts

- an open meeting space fostering collaboration and teamwork

- murals and wall art capturing brand personality and drivers of culture

- a micro-museum, gallery wall, or library dedicated to showcasing the brand's historical moments or products

- a branded space created for personal calls (so staff don't have to go on long walks away from the building to find some privacy)

Engaging Your Team through Artifacts

Great Artifacts are intentionally designed to engage your organization's people in meaningful and tangible ways. It doesn't matter how much money you spend creating the Artifact. What matters is the difference it makes for your people, whether it reinforces your brand, and how it helps them live it out.

Your Key Takeaways

- Artifacts create the topmost layer of your culture. They include tangible, visible objects echoing the deeper layers of your culture.

- Artifacts can be designed to foster a sense of belonging, help staff carry out their work, or engage employees with a greater sense of ownership.

- Upgrade your swag by intentionally designing it to articulate your brand and drive it forward.

- Work with a professional trained in design thinking to create customized, empathetic, and user-centric Artifacts that reinforce your brand.

- Your Artifacts don't need to be complicated or expensive. They simply need to move your people closer to your brand and help them live it out.

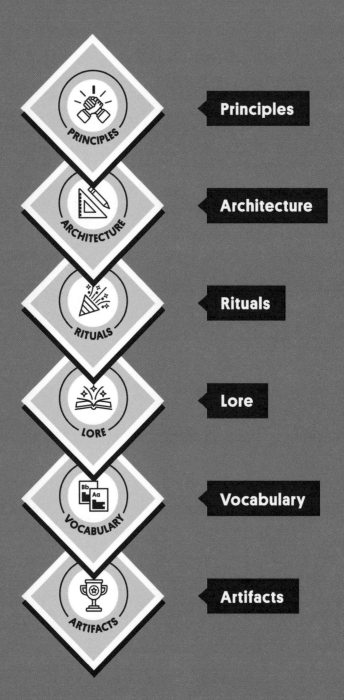

Principles

Architecture

Rituals

Lore

Vocabulary

Artifacts

Conclusion

How your brand operates on the inside matters more than how it looks on the outside. Your organization's internal culture shapes everything your employees do, and it determines whether they consistently deliver on your brand promise to differentiate you from the competition, attract more customers, and turn them into raving fans and loyal followers.

Your culture either ignites your momentum and propels your brand forward—or it falls short of your promise, discredits your marketing, and devours your brand. At the end of the day, your culture is your strategy for success, and it affects your bottom line more than any other dimension of your brand.

Lead with Culture to Lift Your Brand

Moniker Group founder and CEO Ryan Sisson doesn't remember the last time he posted on his brand's Instagram account. Social media falls low on his list of priorities. So does his website. It took him nine years to finally launch a site for the brand's legacy business, Moniker Design Co. But his priorities are purposeful and calculated. "It's not hard for us to decide which to prioritize when it comes to external identity and culture," Sisson says. "It's always culture."[70]

He'd like to put more time and money into building Moniker's external brand identity. But Sisson has always focused first on fostering an authentic culture that engages employees around the brand. That inward focus pays off outwardly. It has infused the brand with the momentum needed to launch eight additional businesses under the Moniker Group label. Today, it's a leading brand consistently delivering elegantly designed and community-centric spaces, experiences, and products.

The genius behind Moniker's operating strategy is that Sisson and his team don't have to prioritize the brand. The culture takes care of

---

70   Ryan Sisson, interview by Ted Vaughn, December 2, 2020.

it for them. "When you have the right culture, it does all the work for you," says Sisson.

The culture Sisson has built naturally brings in the right employees and pushes out those who don't fit. It aligns employee behavior to support the brand. It keeps everyone engaged in the company's core values for prioritizing people, bringing dreams to life, and fostering community. By investing in the culture, his team has cultivated a successful brand that stands head and shoulders above the rest. Despite economic challenges and market changes, Moniker Group continues to outperform the competition, deliver on its brand promise, and make a lasting impact in the community.

Building a Stand-Out Brand from the Inside Out

After reading this book, you now know what it takes to build an organizational culture that accelerates your brand and improves your competitive advantage. With the Marquee Culture method, every dimension of your organization aligns to create an irresistible experience differentiating you from your competitors and attracting dedicated followers. This method gives you a practical road map for integrating your brand into the six distinct yet interconnected layers of culture:

- **Principles.** Principles guide employees with specific ways to live out your brand and consistently deliver on your promise. When tied to clear behaviors, they steer your people to act and make decisions that align with the brand. Accelerate your success by examining your values and recasting them into clear, actionable, brand-building Principles that take your people's performance to the next level.

- **Architecture.** When designed to reflect your brand, your systems and structures set up your employees to experience your organization at its best. Everything from budgets to hiring to decision-making should line up to create seamless employee experiences that trickle down to deliver excellence to your customers. Structure your Architecture like a well-designed building so that it supports your brand purpose simply, organically, and sincerely.

- **Rituals.** Rituals reinforce your values by giving your staff creative opportunities to express what your brand stands for. The brand-building power of Rituals lies in their ability to generate excitement and energy for the people who matter most—your employees. Energize and engage your people with Rituals that help them bring your brand to life.

- **Lore.** The canon of stories circulating within your organization reflects your culture with startling accuracy. These stories reveal your employees' positive, negative, and mundane experiences within your organization. Toxic stories point to the ways your culture is eroding your brand. Cultivate brand-positive Lore by listening to your people, telling on-brand stories, and fostering a culture that reinforces your values and elevates your brand.

- **Vocabulary.** A lexicon of brand-building words and phrases helps your people understand the key concepts driving your brand and how they can move it forward. Vocabulary also points employees to otherwise unseen opportunities for greater impact, innovation, and stand-out performance. Curate a Vocabulary that orients your people to what's most important to your brand.

- **Artifacts.** Comprising the layer of culture closest to the surface, Artifacts are what your people can see, feel, and touch. These physical spaces and tangible objects allow your people to engage with your brand and bring it to life. Create intentionally designed swag and customized Artifacts that resonate with your employees and reinforce your brand.

Harness Your Culture Into a

Brand-Building Powerhouse

It takes hard work to integrate your brand into your culture. Alignment requires focus and endurance to stay the course. It demands ongoing leadership to keep reinforcing the things that matter and engaging employees in an authentic culture. You'll be called upon to lead with heart, courage, and compassion. You and those on your leadership team will need to be brutally honest about the state of your culture, and you may have to make hard decisions to stay true to the brand. But your efforts will pay off. You'll get a more engaged and efficient workforce, industry-leading performance, unbeatable growth, and a differentiated brand that stays ahead of the pack.

It's time to put your know-how into action and begin using the tools in this book to align your brand and culture. Start by gathering your core team, and work together to identify how your culture has blocked your brand's momentum. Bring your culture into the light, and agree to take the steps to infuse it into your brand.

Let us know how it goes. And if you find yourself deep in the weeds and losing your way, contact us. We can help you chart a path forward to kick-start your culture and boost your brand's success.

You've got the tools to harness your culture into a brand-building powerhouse that drives success and outperforms the competition. Now go put them to work. Commit to aligning your culture with your brand, and get ready for your people to push past barriers and help build the brand you only dreamed could be possible.

Mark Miller | mark.m@historicagency.com
PRESIDENT

Ted Vaughn | ted.v@historicagency.com
BRAND STRATEGIST

Historic Agency | www.historicagency.com
610 N. Gilbert Rd. Suite 201, Gilbert, AZ 85234

   @historicagency

Acknowledgments

Mark Miller

First and foremost, thank you to my wife, Sarah, for pushing me to do this book. You encouraged me to step out in faith on this entrepreneurial journey. Every time it got tough, I found you in my corner, pushing me back into the ring to keep fighting. Your support means the world to me. I wouldn't be here without you.

To Max and Penny, thank you for the joy you bring to my life. Always remember you can do anything you work hard at.

Ted, thank you for sharpening all my ideas and replacing the bad ones with good ones. Your partnership has shaped not only Historic, but also me as a leader. You've helped me find my voice and style as a leader and have both challenged and supported me. That has shaped who I am today.

To all the other leaders who took time in their crazy lives to invest in me: Julie Murphree, Houston Clark, Todd Austin, Matt Salley, Matt Samuelson, David and Gary Kinnaman, and Stan Endicott.

To the amazing team I get to lead at Historic, thank you for all the work and support you've given to this book and our small but mighty agency. As an entire team, we are beyond blessed to work with such purposeful and passionate clients. I'm glad I get to share such meaningful work with all of you.

To all our amazing clients over the years, thank you for trusting us with your brand.

Ted Vaughn

Having an idea and turning it into a book while building a business to serve world-changing clients is no easy task. Deep thanks to Mark Miller for working tirelessly on this book and driving it to completion. Over the past nine years, your partnership has been one of the best things to happen to me and, certainly, to my career. To the entire Historic Team for making this book better because of your feedback, talent, and investment: getting to partner with all of you in the meaningful work we do at Historic is a true honor and privilege.

So many profound leaders have shaped my mind and heart over my decades on earth. I wouldn't have been able to write this book without your direct influence and impact on my life. Chris Nichols, Roberta Hestenes, Jim Moriarty, Houston Clark, Stan Endicott, Monty Kelso, Anthony Miller, and Mingo Palacios, to name a few.

To the many clients who have allowed me to "poke under the hood" and contribute to your mission in some meaningful way, this book is a testament to your coachability and partnership. Working with you over the years has been one of the most transformative, educational, and humbling experiences of my career. The list of clients is too long to mention you all, but from Rochester to Dallas to Littleton, this book is the product of your investment and trust.

I'm grateful to the many friends who make my life more fulfilling and joyful. Among the many I could name, Steve and Kristen, Matt and Jessica, Liza and Austin, and Mingo and Fallon have directly shaped this book (and my life). I've learned so much just by living life alongside you.

Most of all, thank you to Licia. You've been a constant source of support, inspiration, stability, and sanity. You're the best editor a guy could ever ask for. Without you, none of this would exist.